AT THE LINE PICKLEBALL: THE WINNING DOUBLES PICKLEBALL STRATEGY

A Shot-by-Shot System for Success

Joe Baker

Written and published by
Joe Baker
First edition
Revised 2022

ISBN-13: 978-1-5399-7285-3
ISBN-10: 1539972852

Library of Congress Control Number: 2016918752

Interior design by Sarah E. Holroyd (https://sleepingcatbooks.com)

CONTENTS

LIST OF FIGURES

PREFACE

The goal of this book is to create a comprehensive instruction on how to play top-level, high-percentage pickleball. I wish I had this guide when I first started playing pickleball about three years ago. The book is a result of all of the information I collected as I tried to develop my pickleball game toward the goal of becoming a viable competitor.

I did not develop the strategy described herein. The approach was in use before I ever heard the word *pickleball*. My main contribution to the sport is trying to capture all of the strategy elements and then organizing them to create this book. I prefer to write the approach in the same shot-by-shot sequence in which the game is played.

I also conducted a very large video analysis study of hundreds of pickleball games in which I looked at each rally shot by shot, logging the data into a spreadsheet. I learned a lot about how top players play the game of pickleball. The analysis also examined average recreational players. From this investigation, I could determine how the pros play the game and assess which shots and strategies were effective and which were not.

ACKNOWLEDGMENTS

I had a lot of help putting together this book. There's no way I could have been successful without the help of some expert instructors: Richard Movsessian, Deb Harrison, and Jeff Shank. These three highly regarded pickleball coaches volunteered to review the manuscript and provide edits and guidance. I appreciate and remain thankful for these coaches' guidance. I am solely responsible for any errors remaining in the book.

Richard Movsessian (Coach Mo)

Coach Mo, perhaps the most popular pickleball coach in the United States, is one of the living legends of the sport. Anyone who has searched the web for pickleball strategy has discovered his guidance. Through his traveling clinics and workshops, he's trained thousands of pickleball players. His pickleballcoach.com website has a nice online strategy guide that has also reached thousands of players. More than 7,700 copies of his *Pickleball Clinics* instructional DVDs have been sold. His instructional guidance is no-nonsense, and the strategy he suggests works for all levels of play.

When I was struggling to move from being a recreational player to a tournament player, Coach Mo concisely explained the rather simple method that the top players were using. As a result, I quickly moved from being a social player to a decent league player. In 2016, Coach Mo gave a clinic to about a hundred pickleball ambassadors at the USA Pickleball Association (USAPA) National Ambassadors Convention to help the ambassadors become better at teaching pickleball.

Coach Mo is more than just a pickleball coach. In 2010, at the age of seventy, Coach Mo and his partner won the silver medal in the thirty-five-plus men's doubles tournament at the USAPA Nationals Pickleball Tournament in Buckeye, Arizona.

Coach Mo taught high school physical education for twenty-nine years in Massachusetts and coached boys' varsity tennis for ten years. He was selected coach of the year in 1979. Coach Mo is a former 4.5-ranked doubles player who played on the 1996 United States Tennis Association (USTA) Florida State Championship 4.5 doubles team. After retiring from teaching, he became a certified member of the United States Professional Tennis Association and became a private teaching professional.

Deb Harrison (Picklepong Deb)

Deb is another living legend of pickleball. A 5.0-rated player, she has won gold and silver medals at the pickleball USAPA Nationals Tournament and the Huntsman World Senior Games in Utah. After teaching tennis for many years, she started playing pickleball in 2004. She's been teaching pickleball for eleven years and operates the Intense Pickleball Camp. She holds a master's degree in sports science from East Stroudsburg College in Pennsylvania. You can learn more about Deb at www.picklepongdeb.com.

Deb is probably best known for her pickleball instructional videos hosted on YouTube. (Search "Deb Harrison" or "Picklepong Deb.") She has more than seventy videos on her YouTube channel. The PBX Club (Pickleball Excellence Club, http://pickleballx.com) lists Deb and Coach Mo among the top three pickleball coaches in the United States.

Jeff Shank

Jeff Shank, a 5.0-rated pickleball player and competitor, is a two-time gold medalist at the USAPA Nationals Tournament. He teaches pickleball clinics in The Villages, Florida, aimed at helping intermediate players progress to becoming advanced players. He created the *100 Strategies* video hosted on YouTube. He chairs the Rules and Officials Program of the Pickleball Community Volunteer Group (PCVG) at The Villages. He's also a player skill-level (rating) assessor.

Jeff operates a pickleball instructional blog (http://pickleballstars. blogspot.com), and he's a contributor to *The Pickleball Show* podcast. He also created the Pickleball Pro Exhibition program to make it easy and economical for folks in The Villages to witness the best pickleball play in the world.

CHAPTER 1—INTRODUCTION

In this book, I'll show you the recipe for winning doubles pickleball that almost all top tournament players use. If you follow this simple shot-by-shot guide, you can bring your game to a very high level very quickly. Where does this recipe come from? All top (5.0 level) pickleball players play what I call at-the-line pickleball. This means playing at the nonvolley zone (NVZ) line, which also means playing as far forward and close to the net as possible.

In brief, the strategy involves moving your team fully forward to the non-volley zone (NVZ) line as quickly as possible and then hopefully playing out the rally while staying at the NVZ line. In addition, the strategy involves trying to keep your opponents away from the NVZ line. As simple as playing at the line sounds, it's more involved than it seems. Getting to the line while your opponents are smacking the ball at your feet can be tough work, and it can all be lost when your opponents hit a clever lob shot.

Why is being fully forward so important? Just like in doubles tennis, being at the net provides the greatest strategic advantage. You have the widest choice of angles and placement positions. You also have the ability to hit down on the ball. In addition, when you and your partner are linked, you can defend your side of the court better than if you are farther back in the court.

In competitive play, you really have no choice but to try to advance to the NVZ line. The statistic is this: if the other team is at the NVZ line and you can't get your team there, then you have a 70 percent chance of losing the rally. It's as simple as this: the team that controls the net controls the match. The team that can get to the NVZ line faster and more reliably and can hold their dominance there longer will win the match. In competitive play, the data clearly bears this out.

To the Social/Recreational Player

Although social pickleball players will definitely benefit from this book, it's especially intended for players who want to advance to the 4.0 skill level or higher. This book will best serve players who seek to play against other at-the-line players. Please do not think that the strategy described in this book does not apply to social play or matches involving opponents who fail to move forward. The strategy described in this book is perfectly applicable to all levels of play, since it addresses how to handle most situations, including circumstances involving deep players, middle-of-the-box players, hard hitters (bangers), and lobbers. Even though you may not choose to play fully forward at the line, this book will still be helpful, since it explains what to do when you are at court locations other than at the line.

I'm going to guess that about 90 percent of pickleball players are social players who have little interest in moving toward tournament play. Most social and recreational players do not play at-the-line pickleball. There are several reasons for this, as follows:

1. They might be scared of being hit at close range. Indeed, at-the-line pickleball rallies usually end with close-range, high-speed action. Intentional shots to the body are fair game. The at-the-line style of play is very aggressive, and it's not for everybody. Periodically, when you play the at-the-line style of play, you'll get hit in the head or face with a fastball. I mainly play outdoors, and the bill of my hat provides some eye protection. Many top players protect their eyes by wearing sunglasses or safety glasses.

2. They may not understand the strategic importance of playing close to the net, or they can't capitalize on it. Part of the reason for being as close to

the net as possible is to seize every smash opportunity that comes your way. If you think that smashing is rude or too rough, then the at-the-line style of play may not be for you.

3. They may feel that their deep-in-the-court game is better than their close-to-the-net game, possibly because they can't react fast enough. However, if you stay back and the other team is up to the NVZ line, then they have more time to react to your shot, and they are in a much better position to hit down on the ball and to hit the ball at your feet. No doubt about it, the at-the-line game requires practice and development of fast reaction time. Backboard wall drills or volleying with a practice partner can dramatically improve reaction time and the development of fast hands.

Note that the at-the-line style of play will not even occur unless all players are committed to playing fully forward and are capable of getting themselves fully forward. For example, the short dinking game (described later) should only occur when all players are fully forward. As you will learn later, whenever a player is not fully forward, you should not invite him or her forward by dinking to him or her. Instead, you should seek to keep him or her away from the NVZ line by placing the ball at foot depth in the court and at a location that requires as much movement or stretching as possible. Likewise, the critical third shot strategy (which will be discussed later) is not relevant if either opponent is not close to the NVZ line, the typical case in social play.

So many aspects of the at-the-line or tournament style of play will likely not get exercised in the social arena. Consequently, you will likely never develop the at-the-line style of play to a high level unless you play against opponents who are good at-the-line players.

Again, please do not think that the strategy described herein does not apply to social play or matches involving opponents who fail to move forward. Certainly, the best strategy in pickleball involves moving your team fully forward to the NVZ line as quickly as possible and trying to keep your opponents away from the NVZ line. As will be discussed later, your choice to play deep in the court handicaps not just you but your partner as well.

However, if you choose to play away from the net, you will use the strategies that apply to midcourt or backcourt positions. So the strategy described in this book will be helpful to all levels of play as it addresses how to handle most situations. It's a comprehensive strategy, addressing about every circumstance. However, some of the strategic elements (e.g., dinking) may not be needed against some types of opponents, such as those who never move very far forward.

The Basis for the Strategy

The basis for the strategy described in this book comes from three fields of study:

First, it involved watching and gathering information from the top pickleball players and coaches. If you watch YouTube videos of the nation's top players, like the finals of the men's open division at the annual USAPA Nationals Tournament events, you will see exactly the strategy described herein.

Second, my approach was to analyze slow-motion videos of thousands of pickleball rallies to gather statistical data on what the top players do and to gather data on what does and does not work. I'm not sure anyone else has done this type of study. A typical study of top-player serves might include collecting the following data for a spreadsheet:

- How deep in the court the serve landed (e.g., 60 percent of service box depth)
- The direction of the serve directed (e.g., to forehand or backhand)
- Approximate serve speed
- Service fault rate (percentage)
- Service return fault rate (percentage)

A typical study of the critical third shot might have much more data:

- What type of shot was played (fastball or soft drop shot)?
- To which player was the third shot directed?
- If the third shot was a soft drop shot, where did it land—in the net, in the kitchen, or beyond the kitchen?
- If the third shot was volleyed back, at what height was it struck—below the net, at net height, above the net, or smash?

- Did a poor third drop shot lead directly to the loss of the rally?
- If the third shot was a fastball, what were the fourth and fifth shots?
- How many shots after the third shot were required to get the serving team to the NVZ line?

Third, developing the strategy involved leveraging the knowledge that has come from a much older and more studied sport: doubles tennis. Pickleball has very little formally collected and published statistical data. In contrast, tennis has published shot-by-shot statistical analysis for at least 261 Grand Slam finals.

Wait a minute. I know what you are thinking. Most tennis players who come to pickleball do it all wrong. They try to play tennis on a pickleball court. They want to hit only fastball ground strokes from the baseline. Indeed, folks from a singles tennis background must be retrained to play doubles pickleball. In singles tennis, the groundstroke low-to-the-net screaming fastball is about the only shot played, and almost all shots are deep to deep.

The strategy is to have the ball outrace your opponent. In doubles tennis, the screaming fastball has a limited but useful place when hitting to deep opponents or trying to make passing shots. As the pickleball court is much narrower than a doubles tennis court, ground stroke passing shots are rarely successful in pickleball. So in doubles pickleball, the screaming ground stroke fastball issued from deep in the court has almost no application. In doubles pickleball, rarely do you play deep player to deep player, and rarely is a passing shot from deep in the court a smart shot.

However, in spite of the differences between doubles tennis and doubles pickleball, many time-tested strategies of doubles tennis do apply to pickleball—just not the frequent use of a screaming fastball. We can't throw out the baby with the bathwater. For example, all of the strategies listed below apply to both doubles pickleball and doubles tennis:

- The ideal strategic arrangement is for you and your partner to play parallel and at the net while keeping your opponents deep in the court. Therefore, your strategy is to get your team to the net while keeping your opponents away from it.

- Toward the strategy of keeping your opponents away from the net, when they are deep, keep them deep by hitting deep shots to them. Likewise, never give them a drop shot they can reach and return, as it provides them an easy journey to the net.
- It's best to hit deep to deep or short (net man) to deep, but you should avoid hitting from deep to short (from deep to a net man). The net man simply has too much strategic advantage compared to any player who is deeper in the court.
- The smash shot is best directed to an unreachable open space. However, if there is no such space, the smash should be directed to the area of the player with the least time to react: the near player, not the deep player.
- When in trouble, go crosscourt (aiming for the center of the tape), but don't hit to a net man. When in big trouble, aim for the center of the tape and lob.
- Don't hit the ball to players. Instead, hit the ball to open spaces to make your opponents run or reach.
- As far as shot depth goes, aim at the depth of your opponent's feet. That is, don't provide a shot that can be volleyed back, and don't provide a shot that bounces well in front of your opponent.
- Always look for the down-the-middle (between your opponents) opportunity, as this is a much higher percentage shot than a down-the-sideline shot.

There are more time-tested and statistically validated doubles tennis strategies that apply to doubles pickleball, and these will be presented later in the book.

It's Not All in Knowing the Strategy

Knowing the at-the-line strategy is only part of what it takes to be a great player. To be great, you also need to have ball-striking and shot-making skills and mobility. In this book, I'll show you how to improve in the areas of strategy, ball striking, and shot making. So, to play great pickleball, you need the following:

Ball-striking skill: This is the ability to consistently get the hit and placement you want—that is, the elimination of flubs, mis-hits, and poor direction control.

Strategy and shot-selection skill: This is where to be and where to place the ball.

Shot-making skill: Above ball-striking skill is shot-making skill. This refers to being able to accurately and consistently make specialty shots that are extremely difficult for your opponents to return. These specialty shots include sharply angled dink shots, lob shots, drop shots, and misdirection shots, among others.

Mobility: It's nearly impossible to play 5.0-level (top-level) pickleball without having great mobility, and it's nearly impossible to play 4.5-level pickleball without having good mobility. However, if you play smart and can develop great ball-striking and shot-making skills, you can be a very good pickleball player even if you have poor mobility.

My Story

One person you will not see if you go to the USAPA Nationals Tournament is me, unless I'm there as a spectator. I'm not a top 5.0-rated player. Nope. I'm a fifty-nine-year-old, overweight recreational player whose knees and hips ache after each outing. If I play more than about six hours per week, I risk getting tendinitis in my knees. Still, I play against Richmond, Virginia's 4.0- to 5.0-rated players every week. I participate in our men's advanced league and compete in local tournaments.

As with many pickleball players, I formerly played tennis, but I had to quit due to the aches and pains. At age fifty-seven, twenty years after playing my last tennis match, by happenstance, I wandered into my church gymnasium when a pickleball game was in progress. They put a paddle in my hand, and I got hooked. I, like most people I know who play pickleball, describe it as, "I immediately became addicted."

I learned the rules and scoring system within a few weeks. As I had the tennis background, I quickly became a good player in the social pickleball arena. Unknown to me, there was a group of about a dozen really good tournament players in Richmond, but I didn't know who they were or where they played. Once I learned of this group, I still had no idea what I needed to do to become competitive. I basically spun my wheels for nearly a year before I discovered and learned the at-the-line system of tournament play.

I figured out this system bit by bit from Richmond's top players and visiting coaches. I also watched YouTube videos, and then I observed and slowed down videos of tournaments involving the top players in the United States. Before publishing this book, I had several of the top coaches in the United States review and edit the manuscript.

Due to my OK-but-not-great mobility and not-so-great reflexes during fast play at the net, I know I'll never be a 5.0-rated player. I'm OK with that, and it doesn't diminish my enjoyment of the sport. In fact, I remain passionate about the game, knowing that my limit will likely be at the 4.0 level or below. Three things drive and motivate me:

- I love competitive play and the camaraderie that is a part of it. I want to beat my buddies, especially my same-age peers, while at the same time enjoy being with them. In league play, I want to climb up the league ladder as far as I can.
- I want to continue to improve my ball-striking and shot-making skills.
- I want to get even better at the strategy—that is, moving correctly, being in the best place, using the best shot technique, and utilizing the right shot, target, and speed.

CHAPTER 2—THE WINNING RECIPE

The Strategy: Where to Be and Where to Place the Ball

The strategy will be discussed in brief here. More discussion on each shot follows later. In brief, among advanced players, a pickleball rally proceeds through the following four phases:

Formality phase: This is the serve and return of serve, followed by the service return team moving up to the nonvolley zone (NVZ) line.

Serving team struggling to get to the NVZ line phase: With a great third shot (drop shot) into the kitchen followed by a fast scramble forward, the serving team can sometimes get to the NVZ line before the fourth shot is made. Usually, getting fully to the NVZ line will require the serving team to make another shot or two into the kitchen before they can get fully to the NVZ line.

Dinking phase: This is the cautious, keep-the-ball-low phase. Dink, dink, dink until someone makes a mistake.

Fast game phase: If the ball gets too high during the dinking phase, a fast volley game will ensue.

Shot #1: The Serve

Player Positions

At the start of the game, the player positions should be as shown in figure 2-1. The server and the server's partner should both be behind the baseline. Make sure you and your partner wait behind the baseline until your opponent hits the service return shot before moving into the court. If you step into the court when serving, move back behind the baseline after making the serve. A big mistake is moving forward too early and then retreating to field a shot.

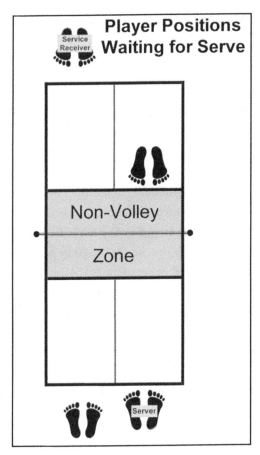

Figure 2-1. Player positions for the serve

An ideal serve, if it can be made consistently, is fast and deep and usually directed at the receiver's backhand. However, not faulting is key. So for most beginner and intermediate players, the best serving strategy is to aim for the center of the box and to minimize serving faults. Serves need not be fast or very low to the net. I suggest using enough arc to easily clear the net by at least eighteen inches. If you aim for the center, your outcome or capability pattern will likely be similar to that shown in figure 2-2. Until you get really consistent, do not attempt to serve fast or deep, and do not attempt to add spin. Just focus on hitting the target: the middle of the box.

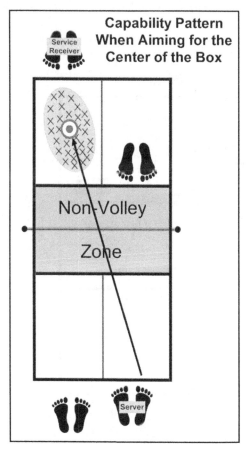

Figure 2-2. Capability pattern

Many players have developed spin serves that work well against their playing peers. So long as you are sure that your winner serves outnumber your service faults, stay with your winning ways. As you progress toward better opponents, you will likely find that spin serves do not help your game. Unlike in tennis, among advanced players, rallies are rarely won on a serve. Even though the ideal serve would be fast and deep with lots of spin, most top players choose to hit rather conservative serves that essentially guarantee that they will not end in fault. My study of hundreds of top 5.0-level serves shows that the top players' serves average landing 54 percent of the way toward the back of the box. See figure 2-3. The serve is discussed in more detail later in this book.

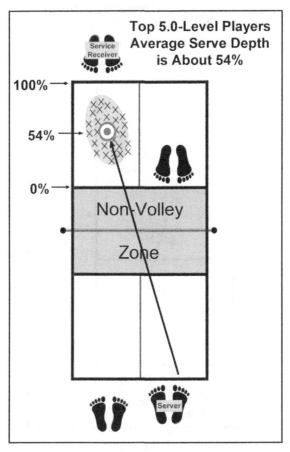

Figure 2-3. Top players' average serve depth

Shot #2: The Return of Serve
Player Positions

The player returning the serve should typically be eighteen to thirty inches behind the baseline. His or her partner should be fully up to the NVZ line with his or her feet only one to two inches behind the NVZ line. The partner of the service receiver should turn his or her upper body to carefully watch whether the serve is in bounds. For serves that land close to the baseline, it's often difficult for the service return player to make the call.

There are two strategy goals of the return of serve, the second shot of the game:

First, the return of serve must allow you to get fully to the NVZ line before the ball comes back to you. For folks with poor mobility, this may require that the return of serve be a lob or semilob. The importance of getting fully to the NVZ line on time is discussed in more detail later.

Second, an ideal return of serve should seek to make the critical third shot as difficult as possible. The ideal shot would be fast and deep with lots of spin. However, the top players choose to hit service return shots that essentially guarantee that these shots will not end in fault. Therefore, the return of serve does not need to be fast. In fact, an arcing, rather slow shot is fine so long as you can hit the middle of the box or deeper. My study of hundreds of top 5.0-level return-of-serve shots shows that the top players' return of serve shots average landing 52 percent of the way toward the back of the serving box. Most coaches agree that the return of serve should be as deep as possible without risking going out of bounds. A bad return is one that is short with a high bounce, as might happen with a high arcing shot that is short. Such a shot can invite a close-range fastball return that could be difficult to handle. In addition, a short return will likely give your opponent an easy journey to the net.

If you don't know your opponents, a good place to aim initially is shown in figure 2-4, as it usually forces a backhand return for a right-handed player. Notice that the target is well away from the baseline and only slightly away from the very center of the non-kitchen area.

However, in tournament play, you need to quickly assess which opponent is less skillful with the rather tricky third shot and then direct all service

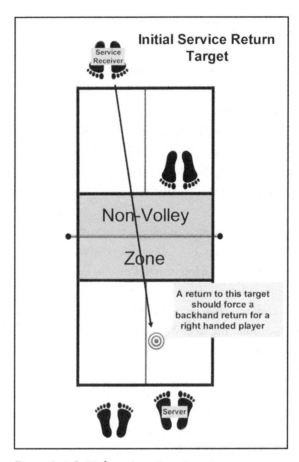

Figure 2-4. Initial service return target

returns to this player. A player who can't reliably make a strategic third shot is a major weakness. The third shot will be discussed later. As with the serve, you can hit your return deeper by hitting it higher rather than harder. Again—and this is an important point—the serve and return-of-serve shots need not be low to the net or fast. Avoid returning the serve with a singles tennis–style low-to-the-net fastball because such shots are more likely to go into the net or out of bounds than yield a benefit. Attempts to add topspin will likely hurt more often than help.

When returning the serve, the service receiver should follow the path of the ball he or she has hit as he or she is moving toward the net. See figure 2-5.

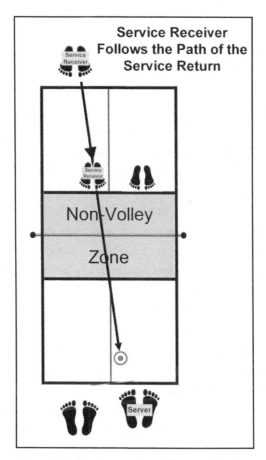

Figure 2-5. Service receiver follows path of service return

The return of serve is discussed in more detail later in this book.

The Service Return Team Claims the Net

Immediately after returning the serve, charge to the NVZ line and be fully ready and in place to receive your opponent's shot, which is the third shot. After hitting the return-of-serve shot, the service receiver must get fully to the NVZ line in time to receive the third shot (the return of the return of serve). Being the first team to seize the net is a vital strategic move. Getting fully to the NVZ line means getting set in position with your toes only an inch or two behind the NVZ line. In addition, you should be slightly compressed, as in a basketball-ready position. A slight forward lean helps allow you to reach your paddle across the line to get shots that are slightly inside the NVZ area.

Both members of the service receiving team must be fully to the NVZ line before the third shot is returned. There are no exceptions to this rule. If you have poor mobility, return the serve with a lob shot if necessary to ensure you get fully to the line on time. Another option to buy time is to return the serve crosscourt. Remember, when at the NVZ line, you need to have your toes only one inch behind the line.

Here's why this fast movement to the NVZ line is so important:

The team at the net has a huge strategic advantage over opponents who are in the backcourt. Net players have more angles and shot placement options than players who are deep in the court, and they can defend their court better than players who are deep.

A beauty of being at the net is that the net shields your feet. In other words, your feet are hidden behind the net, and your opponent will have difficulty hitting the ball at your feet. When you are near the net, almost any flub or mis-hit you make will still go back across the net. Getting to the net gives you a chance to smash any ball coming high. In advanced play, you can't forgo winning opportunities and expect to win. Even if the ball is not high, being at the net allows you to quickly send it back to limit your opponent's ability to move forward toward the net.

Being at the net in time to receive the third shot forces your opponent to play a critical third shot where he or she has a huge disadvantage, hitting from deep in the court to a team at the net. Therefore, getting your team to the NVZ line immediately after returning the serve now forces your opponent to do one of three things:

1. He or she can play a drop shot into the kitchen, a rather tough shot. This is generally the best strategy, and the top players use it at least 80 percent of the time. However, even for top players, such drop shots fail and directly lead to a loss of the rally 15–20 percent of the time they are attempted.

2. He or she can play a fastball or other shot that the net players can volley back. While a fastball can sometimes be a winner, the fastball usually gets

directed back to foot depth, and then the serving team must play another shot from no man's land (the court area outside of the kitchen).

3. He or she can play a defensive lob. Lob shots from the baseline usually do not work well against advanced players who have good mobility. There's too much time to move and react. While lob shots do not work well against advanced players, they can work well against players who have poor mobility, especially when playing indoors where wind is not a factor.

So there's no easy option when players who are deep in the court are facing skilled players at the net. The statistics are as follows. When the serving team makes the third shot of the game (the return of the return of serve) from deep in the court against net players, this shot alone has at least a 17 percent chance of directly causing the loss of the rally for the serving team, usually by the ball going into the net or getting smashed back.

The 17 percent statistic comes from an analysis of top 5.0-level players. The figure jumps to 27 percent for 4.5-level players. Note that this advantage of the service return team can only be realized if both of their members are fully up to the NVZ line in time to receive the third shot. In other words, they must employ the advantage of being at the net to gain the statistical advantage. Let me also add that it's extremely annoying to play with a partner who does not get to the line on time, because you are giving away your 17–27 percent advantage.

Remember, if you have poor mobility, hit a lob or semilob shot for the return of serve. Figure 2-6 shows why it's critical to get fully to the NVZ line versus hanging back even slightly.

Therefore, if you fail to get your team to the NVZ line following the return of serve, your opponent need not attempt to make a drop shot into the kitchen. Instead, he or she can hit a much easier shot, usually designed to land at foot depth in your court and midway between you and your partner. So, if you fail to be at the NVZ line in time, the 17–27-plus-percent advantage you have is eliminated.

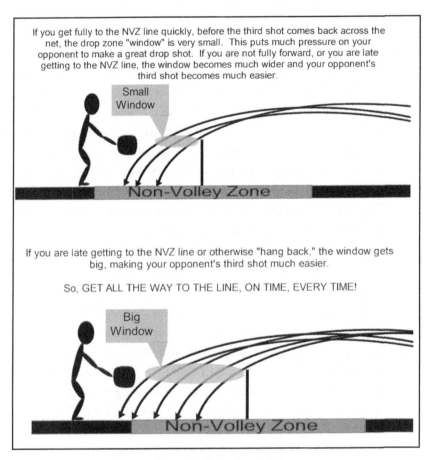

Figure 2-6. Why it is critical to get fully to the NVZ line

Other Problems with Failure to Get to the NVZ Line on Time
Lost Opportunity

Here's another problem that happens from service receivers hanging back or otherwise being out of position to receive the third shot. This failure to get dominance of the net will likely lead to the other team getting the first dominance of the net. If you hang back, your opponent will hit deep to you to keep you back, and then he or she will scramble forward to the net. So if you forgo your opportunity to be the first team to the net, you will likely incur a struggle to get there later.

Avoiding Dysfunctional Court Positioning

Coaches agree that the playing partners need to stay linked together and need to play parallel and as forward as possible. The one-up-one-back arrangement yields both poor offense and defense. In such an arrangement, the forward player can't see his or her partner (where he or she is or what he or she can cover). With an open net position, your opponent is no longer required to keep the ball low and in the kitchen.

Instead, a smart opponent will aim for the deep player's exposed feet. Smash opportunities at the unmanned net position will be lost. As for the penalty for the defense, an uncovered area exists between the forward and back players. In addition, deep positioning yields diminished court protection capability.

Shot #3: The Third Shot

Let's assume your opponent made a great return of the serve and is now with his or her partner fully up to the NVZ line (as fully up to the net as possible). In other words, the second shot landed deep in your territory, and you now face two opponents at the net. Your goal is to get your team to the net as quickly as possible. The statistic is this: when you are facing a team at the net, if you can't get your own team to the net, you have a 70 percent chance of losing the point. So at this point in the rally, unless you have a great scoring opportunity, your priority should be to get your team to the NVZ line.

The ideal third shot is a drop shot into the NVZ, also known as the kitchen. This soft drop shot is the one that the top players play more than 75 percent of the time. As you execute such a shot, you and your teammate should quickly scramble toward the NVZ line. The rather slow drop shot described allows you more time to scramble forward than a fastball would. Among advanced 5.0-level players, a drop shot into the kitchen followed by a fast scramble forward to the net will get the serving team fully forward to the net in time to receive the fourth shot about 54 percent of the time. When they fail to get fully forward after their first drop shot, they usually succeed after their next drop shot attempt.

Not getting to the NVZ line quickly will mean that the serving team will play the fourth shot in no man's land (the area of the court outside of the kitchen). Remember, the purpose of the rather difficult third shot drop shot is to allow you to move forward toward the net. Therefore, don't hit this shot and then stand in place admiring it. Instead, hit it and then use the forward momentum of the strike to carry you forward. As with most shots where you intend to move forward, follow the path of the ball to the net.

If you are making the third shot, your partner should advance forward a couple steps to get a head start toward the NVZ line. If the third shot (drop shot) is too high, it will probably be volleyed back. You and your partner will need to stop and split-step to field the volleyed return.

Two great targets for the third shot are shown in figure 2-7.

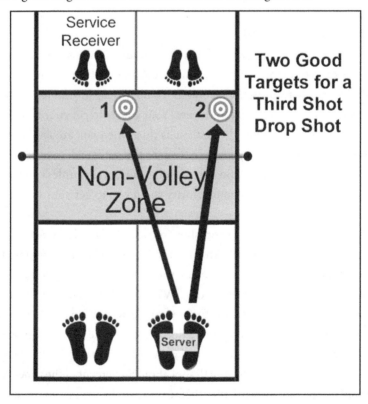

Figure 2-7. Two good targets for a third shot (drop shot)

About the best thing you can do for your game is to learn how to make drop shots into the kitchen. The sooner you learn how to do this, the better off you will be. You will not advance very far in the game without being able to get shots into the kitchen. Not only do you use this drop shot for the third shot, you also use it whenever you have to hit up on the ball and you are facing two opponents at the net.

The statistical data on the importance of the third shot and getting your team fully forward quickly is overwhelming. A review of more than thirty tournament games shows that the team with the best third shot success percentage will be the winning team about 75 percent of the time. Third shot success means that the serving team was able to get to the NVZ line after the third shot or within a shot or two after the third shot. Drills for learning this shot are described later in this book.

A bad third shot drop shot will either go too deep, allowing a volley return, or it will go too short and hit the net. Obviously, it's better to be too long than too short. Players at the 3.5–4.0 level are more likely to fail by going into the net than 5.0-level players will. Top players more often err on the side of too deep than too short by about a three-to-one ratio.

Now let's suppose that one or both of your opponents fails to get to the NVZ line following their return of the serve. In such a case, you should not execute the rather difficult drop shot into the kitchen. There are two reasons for avoiding the drop shot in this case:

First, the shot has a rather high failure rate (going into the net or getting smashed back).

Second, you should never invite your opponent to move forward toward the net. Instead, you should seek to keep him or her back or push him or her back. So if your opponents are not at the net, your goal should be to keep them back. To do this, you should attempt to place the ball at the left-heel target of the deeper opponent. See figure 2-8.

21

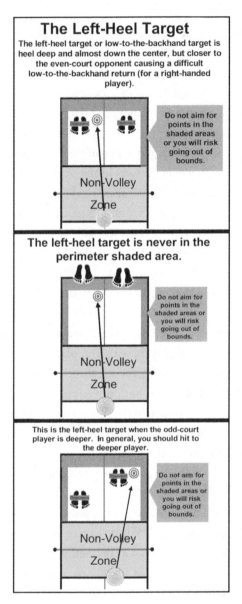

Figure 2-8. The left-heel target

We will refer to the left-heel target many times in this book because it is perhaps the most important target in the game of pickleball. Note that the left-heel target is not always exactly right at the left heel. More often, it's heel

For a right-handed player, shots that land outside the left heel are nearly impossible to field.

Figure 2-9. A difficult shot

deep and down the center between your opponents but closer to the even-court opponent, causing a difficult low-to-the-backhand return (for a right-handed player). Immediately upon hitting this shot, you and your partner should scramble to the NVZ line to establish dominance at the net.

It's rare that you need to hit a fastball ground stroke in pickleball. However, a situation where it's useful is when your opponent returns the serve and then makes the beginner mistake of staying back deep in the court. Let's say his or her partner is midway up to the NVZ line and thus could poach. The goal is to send a shot deep to the player who is deep (the service return player in this case). You have to avoid a possible poach. A great shot is a rather fast, low-to-the-net shot that the possible poacher can't reach. See figure 2-10.

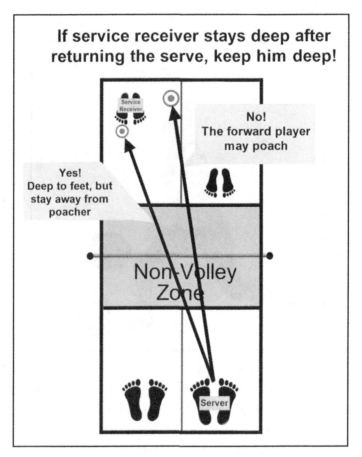

Figure 2-10. Keep-the-service-receiver-back shot

In social play, you will likely not need to play the difficult drop shot into the kitchen because your opponents will likely not be fully forward. If both opponents are in the middle of the court, play a shot to the left-heel target, as shown in figure 2-11. So, aim for heel deep in the court, approximately centered between your opponents but closer to the even-court player to ensure he or she takes it and plays a low-to-the-backhand shot. Note that when making this shot to the left-heel target, it's better to err too short than too deep, which gives your opponent a volley shot.

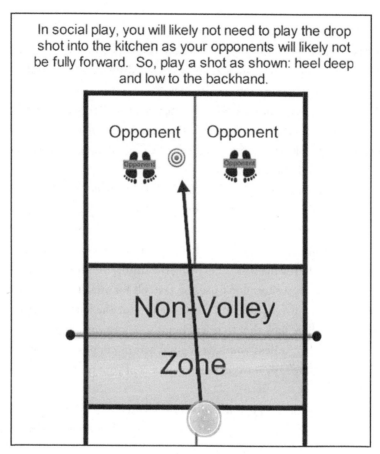

In social play, you will likely not need to play the drop shot into the kitchen as your opponents will likely not be fully forward. So, play a shot as shown: heel deep and low to the backhand.

Figure 2-11. The left-heel target when both opponents are in no man's land

Fastball/Block Shot/Drop Shot (Bullet, Block, Drop)

Among top players, the drop shot into the kitchen is the most frequently used third shot strategy. Another less-often-used third shot strategy is to hit a low fastball down the center and hope to get a defensive blocking shot response that leaves the ball in about midcourt position. From here, you can hit a rather easy drop shot into the kitchen, allowing you to get to the NVZ line. The bullet/block/drop strategy is best employed when the return of serve is not deep and comes right to your forehand.

There are pros and cons to this strategy:

Pros: You can get outright winners from fastballs, whereas you can rarely get a winner from a drop shot. Also, making a drop shot from midcourt is easier than making one from the baseline.

Cons: With speed comes loss of control, and fastballs often go into the net or out-of-bounds deep. Also, if the fastball can be handled with something better than a blocking shot, you might get the fastball directed to a place you can't reach or right back at your feet.

If an opponent frequently uses a fastball as his or her third shot, it will be important for you to avoid returning out-balls (shots that will go out of bounds). Likewise, if your opponent can't judge out-balls but instead tries to return everything, you may be able to use the fastball/block shot/drop shot strategy to get to the net instead of using the third shot (drop shot).

As with the drop shot, don't use the fastball for your third shot if your opponents are not fully forward. Instead, aim for the left-heel target, and send over a rather slow shot that will bounce before your opponent hits it. Why? Remember, unless you have a good scoring opportunity, your goal at this point in the rally is to get both members of your team fully forward.

Short Return of Serve/Fastball Down the Center

When a return of serve is very short—and especially if it has a high bounce and comes to your forehand—this is a great time to hit a fastball as a third shot. If the opponent team is not tightly linked, this makes the opportunity even better. Down the center is usually a great place to aim such a fastball. The fast game is discussed in more detail later in this book.

Lob Shot Third Shot

My studies of hundreds of rallies show that using the lob as a third shot strategy is low percentage play. This finding applies to all levels of play. Only in the rather rare case of a great lobber playing against a poor lob handler can the percentage become acceptable. However, you may need to use a lob shot if a return-of-serve shot gets you in trouble.

Shot #4: Play the Fourth Shot to Hinder Opponent Forward Progress

Let's assume your opponent made a great drop shot into the kitchen on the third shot of the game. Your opponents are smartly scrambling toward the net after hitting the soft drop shot. Unless they are extremely fast, they probably will not get fully to the NVZ line by the time you are ready to hit the fourth shot. In other words, they are caught in no man's land.

If such is the case, if the third shot is about centered and if both opponents are about the same depth back, the best strategy is to hit a shot to the left-heel target of the even-court opponent. I call this the keep-them-back shot. See figure 2-12. Such shots are awkward to hit, and they help stymie forward progress. If your opponent returns your shot, he or she can likely follow it to be fully established at the NVZ line before the fifth shot is made.

Now let's assume your opponent made a great drop shot into the kitchen on the third shot of the game and your opponents moved all the way to the NVZ line in time to receive the fourth shot. In such a case, unless you see a hole between them, you should play a dink shot.

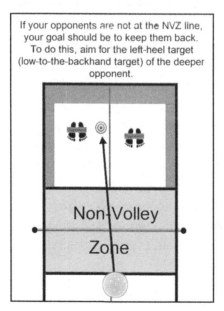

Figure 2-12. The keep-them-back shot

Now let's assume your opponent's third shot came in a little high but not high enough to smash. See figure 2-13. If at all possible, take it in the air (volley it back) versus letting it bounce, and aim for the left-heel target. This is a volley version of the keep-them-back shot. Be sure to keep this shot low and unable to be volleyed back. Remember the rule: never give your opponent a ball in the air (a ball he or she can volley back) unless it is intended to defeat his or her reaction time or it's a deep lob. Taking the ball in the air versus letting it bounce helps minimize your opponent's forward progress.

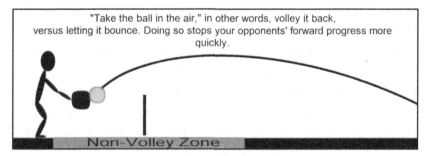

Figure 2-13. *When keeping them back, take the ball in the air*

If the third shot comes to a sideline and you are at the net, you may direct it back down the sideline to foot depth, but ensure you leave a margin for error. See figure 2-14. These shots are especially good if your near opponent is too close to the center or fails to stop and split-step.

When dinking, it's OK to hit toward a kitchen sideline. When trying to hit a drop shot into the kitchen, it's OK to hit toward a kitchen sideline. However, long shots directed toward sidelines outside the kitchen have too much risk of going out of bounds and are low-percentage shots. Top players rarely attempt such long shots. See figure 2-15.

Continue to prevent your opponent's progress toward the net as long as possible. Be patient with this process, and avoid making risky shots. With luck, your opponents will die in no man's land (fault before ever getting to the NVZ line).

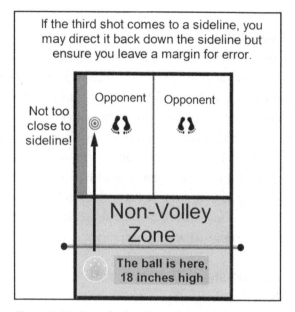

Figure 2-14. Fourth shot down the sideline

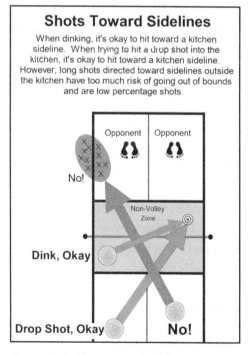

Figure 2-15. Shots toward sidelines

Fielding a Fastball Third Shot

Now let's suppose the third shot is a fastball. In such a case, the service return player may not be fully to the NVZ line. In such a case, the partner of the service return player should field all shots in the center area, even those that are on his or her partner's side of the center line. The return of the fastball will depend on your skill. A great return of the fastball would be to the left opponent's left-heel target, in an attempt to jam him or her. Another great return, provided you have opponents with poor mobility, would be a dink, angled to create a long distance between the ball and your opponent. If you don't have the capabilities described above, just block the shot to go left of the center line toward the left player's backhand.

Fielding the Fourth Shot

We've just talked about how to play a fourth shot. Now let's talk about how to handle them. Let's say you've made a great third shot (drop shot). You and your partner are now charging forward. First, you must stay linked to your partner so the defensive wall is intact and properly positioned according to the ball position. (This wall is discussed more in chapter 3.) A common and serious fault is to charge while leaving a gap between you and your partner. Remember, converge on the path of the ball.

Next, you and your partner must stop, split-step, and get compressed into a basketball-like ready position before the fourth shot comes across the net to you. Trying to hit while moving usually results in a bad shot. Moving forward into a ball directed at your feet will almost certainly cause failure. I call this getting jammed. If you are stopped and compressed in a split-step position, you can field just about any shot coming to you, even if it's coming at your feet. See figure 2-16. If you were unsuccessful in getting fully forward after your third shot drop shot, you should continue to make drop shot attempts until you get fully forward.

Review of the First Four Shots

Let's go through a quick review of how the first four shots of pickleball are played when they are played smartly and successfully:

It's nearly impossible to field shots aimed at your feet if you are standing straight up or if you are running forward.

However, if you are stopped and compressed in split-step, you can field the shots that are aimed at your feet.

No way! No way! Yes!

Figure 2-16. The value of being compressed in split-step

1. When serving, seek to reduce service faults as your first priority. It's OK to just aim for the middle of the box. Slow and high serves are OK. Fast and deep serves are great so long as you can deliver them with consistency.

2. Initially, the return of serve is made to the point shown in figure 2-4, forcing a backhand return. As soon as you discover which opponent has less skill with the third shot, send all return-of-serve shots to this person. Again, a key is to avoid losing this point. Deep returns are ideal, but it's OK for beginner/intermediate players to just aim for the middle of the service boxes. Return the serve crosscourt or with a semilob, if necessary, to ensure you can get to the line on time. After hitting this shot, both players advance fully to the NVZ line in time to receive the third shot.

3. When both opponents are fully forward, the third shot is a drop shot into the NVZ. Hopefully, it goes to a player's backhand. Both players follow the third shot, making as much forward progress as possible.

4. The fourth shot is a dink, if both opponents get to the net. If they did not and if the ball is centered in the court, the fourth shot is the keep-them-back shot. It goes down the middle and low to the left player's backhand to stymie his or her forward progress. The serving team may need to make several drop shot attempts in their struggle to get fully forward.

5. Once all players are at the NVZ line, a defensive dinking game begins.

Additional Comments

These two things can usually predict the outcome of advanced-level play, the first being the most important:

1. When serving, how well did the team do in getting to the NVZ line quickly and reliably?

This entails making the third shot drop shot reliably and then quickly scrambling forward. The third shot drop shot is difficult. Even the pros can only land these drop shots in the kitchen about 54 percent of the times they try. But when they fail, they usually fail by being just a little too deep, thereby keeping the point alive. Serving teams that can't reliably get forward will quickly lose their status as servers and thereby their ability to make points.

2. When receiving, how well did the team do in getting to the NVZ line quickly, and how well did they do in stopping the progress of the other team in coming forward?

This means returning the serve and then getting fully forward before the third shot comes across the net. This forces the opponent to play the critical third shot. Indeed it's difficult and intimidating to hit a drop shot toward two tall opponents who are pinned at the NVZ line. It also means reaching into the kitchen to volley the third shot back, if possible. Stopping opponent progress also means hitting keep-them-back shots that keep the opponent team as deep as possible for as long as possible.

Chapter 2 Quiz
Serving Strategies

Q1: You are serving to the even-court opponent, and you have trouble making third shot drop shots with your backhand. What do you do?

A1: When serving to the even-court opponent, stand as close to the center as possible. That way, almost any return coming to your side of the court will give you a forehand shot. Likewise, when serving to the odd-court opponent, stand as close to the corner as possible. That way, almost any return coming to your side of the court will give you a forehand shot.

Return-of-Serve Strategies

Q1: Your even-court opponent returned the serve very short to the center of the court and only four feet behind the NVZ line. The service return man is smartly scrambling forward. What should you do?

A1: A safe, conservative, and rather easy shot from this range would be a drop shot into the kitchen. If you are quick and can get in place, another option would be a low-to-the-net, rather fast shot aimed just enough off center to force a reaching low backhand volley return from the even-court player who is not fully forward. With this, you may get an outright winner or a weak return that leads to a winner. Just make sure you don't hit this shot too hard such that it goes out of bounds. If the opponent fails to stop and split-step, you may also jam him or her or get the ball past him or her without it being touched.

If you have poor mobility and have to field a very short return, you will likely be hitting on the run (hitting while still moving). Hitting on the run often causes the ball to go into the net. So if you are struggling to get to the ball, play a soft and safe shot, and go crosscourt, which will buy you the most time to recover.

Comment: If you get in this situation where you've made a weak return to the middle, you and your partner need to merge toward the center line to prevent a hole. Make sure your paddle is up and you are in a split-step, compressed, ready position.

Q2: Your opponent returned the serve very short toward the odd-court sideline and only five feet behind the NVZ line. The service return man is smartly scrambling forward. What should you do?

A2: A safe, conservative, and rather easy shot from this range would be a drop shot into the kitchen. Another option would be a low-to-the-net, rather fast shot aimed at the near opponent's right side that forces a paddle flip to the forehand position (for a right-handed player). With this, you will likely get a weak return. Just make sure you don't hit this shot too wide or deep.

Comment: If you get in this situation where you've made a weak return to the sideline, make sure you can cover the down-the-line fastball shot. Your partner needs to slide to the center line to prevent a hole. Make sure your paddle is up and you are in a split-step, compressed, ready position. As your opponent will be near a sideline, look for a chance to return the ball through a gap between your opponents.

Third-Shot and Fourth-Shot Strategies

Q1: Your opponent's third shot is a strong forehand, low-to-the-net, screaming fastball right down the middle. What do you do?

A1: If the shot is low and fast, you may only be able to block the shot, which isn't bad. Block it to the left-heel target, if possible. A better shot would be a dink, perhaps angled to a sideline, which would likely be a winner. A great skill to have is being able to dink back an incoming fastball. Use a backboard to practice this skill. Hit a fastball to the board and then dink your next shot. Better yet, get with a practice partner to learn how to dink an incoming fastball.

Q2: Your opponent's third shot drop shot landed in the kitchen, near the T in the center of the court. Both opponents are scrambling forward, but they are too slow to get to the NVZ line before your shot goes to them. What shot should you make, assuming you can't volley the shot back?

A2: Go for the left-heel target of the (right-handed) left player, as described earlier. However, be careful not to provide your opponent an easy volley shot. By the way, if you receive a mid-court "keep them back shot" to your forehand that you can volley, this could be a good time to issue a fastball. If there is a gap between your opponents, go for it.

Q3: Your opponent's third shot (drop shot) landed in the kitchen, near the odd-court sideline. Both opponents are scrambling forward. What should you do, assuming you can't volley the shot back?

A3: You have several choices. As you are at the net, you may hit down the sideline, especially if your opponent is biased too far toward the center and especially if he or she continues his or her forward motion as you are hitting. You may also go for the left-heel target, which is almost always a good choice. You could also make a sharp crosscourt shot.

Q4: Your opponent's third shot (drop shot) landed in the kitchen, near the even-court (deuce-court) sideline, giving you a forehand shot. Both opponents are scrambling forward. What should you do, assuming you can't volley the shot back?

A4: As you are at the net, you may hit down the sideline, especially if your opponent is biased too far toward the center and especially if he or she continues his or her forward motion as you are hitting. Of course you can go for the left-heel target of the near opponent.

Q5: Your opponent's third shot (drop shot) came over the center of the net a little high, and it's headed straight for your feet. Both opponents are scrambling forward. What should you do?

A5: When you are up to the line, compressed, and leaning slightly forward, you can volley back shots that are headed for your feet. You should never let a third shot bounce when you can volley it back because you should stop your opponents' forward progression as quickly as possible. So volley the shot back to the left player's left-heel target with as much pace as you can safely apply. Do not provide a shot he or she can volley back. Remember, when they are back, keep them back. Unless you are playing against opponents with poor mobility, do not try short shots. Unless your opponents are at or near the NVZ line, I would not try shots to the sidelines because the risk of going out of bounds exceeds any benefit.

Q6: Your third shot was lousy, way too high, setting up your opponent to make a smash. What do you do?

A6: You and your partner need to both stay back and try to field the smash. If you can field the smash, your best shot may be a lob over the center of the net. Aim for the center of the non-kitchen area. If this lob is short, allowing another smash, repeat with another lob. If you can get a deep lob and you see that your opponent is going to allow it to bounce, you and your partner should rush to the NVZ line.

Comment: It's very difficult to receive a fast smash and then make a drop shot into the kitchen. However, if you have this skill, indeed use it.

Q7: Your rather slow-moving opponent in the even court has returned your serve with a fastball. He's lumbering up to the NVZ line, but because he hit a fastball, he will be only halfway to the NVZ line by the time your shot (the third shot) comes over. Where do you aim to place your third shot?

A7: You should aim for your slow-moving opponent's feet, being careful to stay away from a down-the-middle shot to prevent a poach from the opponent already at the net. Remember, don't try to hit the rather difficult drop shot into the kitchen when you have an opponent who is away from the NVZ line.

Q8: You hit a good third shot drop shot that landed in the kitchen. You did a good job of quickly following the shot, making as much forward progress toward the NVZ line as possible. However, you did not get fully forward. The fourth shot is headed toward your feet. What do you do with the fourth shot?

A8: In general, you should continue to make drop shots until you can get fully forward. Whenever you are facing a properly linked opponent team located at the net and you have to hit up on the ball, hit a slow shot designed to drop into the kitchen. Unless you see a big hole or put-away opportunity, your first priority should be getting your team to the NVZ line, and you do this by scrambling forward after hitting drop shots.

CHAPTER 3—NET PLAY

Learn to Dink and Avoid Giving the Other Team a Shot

Suppose all four players are now properly positioned at the NVZ line. At this close range, about the worst thing you can do is provide your opponent a ball that he or she can smash. Instead, you need to be very careful, which creates the dinking game. So instead of carelessly giving your opponent a ball in the air (a ball that can be volleyed back) that can invite a smash, you should provide shots that essentially prevent such aggression.

Therefore, you should produce dink shots that land in or near the NVZ and require your opponent to hit up on the ball. In other words, feed your opponent dink shots that he or she can't do anything with offensively. It's usually unwise to give your opponent a ball in the air.

Priority-wise, your dinking game should develop as follows:

1. Get positioned correctly, and stay there. This is discussed more below. You must also stay linked to your partner, never more than six to seven feet away from your partner to form a wall. Slide and reposition the wall after each hit of the ball. See figure 3-2.

2. Reduce flubs and mis-hits that usually go into the net. Flubs normally result from hitting the ball outside of the paddle sweet spot (hitting off-center). Flubs or mis-hits often result from not watching the ball. Practice watching the ball by hitting with a practice partner or against a wall.

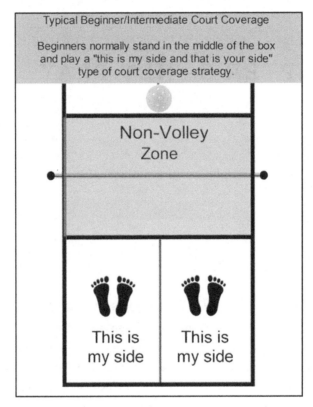

Figure 3-1. Typical beginner coverage strategy

3. Get the ball over the net reliably but not so high that your opponent can volley it back. Again, practice with a partner or use a practice wall.

4. Learn to steer dink shots left and right. Again, practice with a partner or use a practice wall.

5. Learn the safe targets and dinking locations to avoid. See figure 3-3. In particular, avoid dinking directly to the opponent opposite you and especially avoid hitting it to this opponent's forehand.

6. Break the defensive wall or stress it to cause a pop-up. To do this, you must be able to steer the ball accurately.

Before we go further with dinking, let's talk about some teamwork skills needed for dinking.

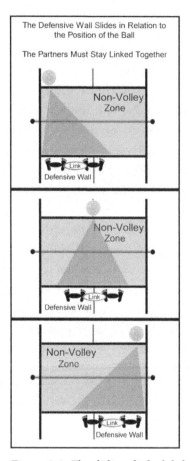

Figure 3-2. The sliding, linked defensive wall

Coverage Teamwork: The Defensive Wall and Importance of Staying Linked to Your Partner

A common fault among beginning players is that they play a "this side is my side and that side is your side" coverage strategy. This is shown in figure 3-1. In this way, player A mainly stays in the middle of his or her box and attempts to defend his or her half of the court, and player B mainly stays in the middle of his or her box and attempts to defend his or her half of the court.

The problem with this is that there is a hole in the center and the hole gets bigger whenever player A or B moves toward a sideline. With such a coverage strategy, it's easy for your opponent to score. As soon as somebody moves toward a sideline, the ball will be placed right down the middle.

Now let's talk about how good players cover the court. Instead of working independently, the teammates link together to form a wall, which slides in relation to the position of the ball. This is shown in figure 3-2. If the ball goes back and forth crosscourt, this involves back-and-forth repositioning. Notice how the teammates stay linked together, not more than about seven feet apart and often closer. Because they can't protect the entire twenty-foot width of the court, they try to protect the most vital part of the width that is near the ball location.

Particularly important is protecting the gap between the two players. Protecting this gap is essential during net play. If your opponents can successfully make down-the-middle shots, you and your partner are likely too far apart. Notice that when the ball is in front of you, you must protect the near sideline, and your partner must protect the middle. Likewise, when the ball is in front of your partner, he or she must protect his or her sideline, and you must protect the middle.

Figure 3-3. Protect against the down-the-middle shot

Beginner teams, even if they understand staying linked, still usually play too far apart. They can't accept leaving part of the court unprotected. When you and your partner are too far apart, even if you do get the down-the-middle shot, the long stretch to get it usually yields a weak, popped-up return. Smart play involves playing by percentages. So do the high-percentage action of protecting the middle, while providing your opponent a low-percentage shot to the unprotected area.

Coverage Teamwork: Communication

Some things you have to do to get really good at pickleball take a lot of work and skill, such as learning how to perform third shot drop shots. However, some things you have to do to be really good are easy, such as communicating well with your partner.

Communication isn't just about good manners. Instead, it's about points and wins instead of losses. Remember, most pickleball games are close, and winning teams may win only a few more rallies than the losing teams. So it pays to do easy things that will help you win.

Pregame Communications

1. If not already known, ask or advise your partner about opponent strengths and weaknesses. Issues such as poor mobility, inferior dinking ability, poor lobbing skills, slow hands, and poor third shot capability should be communicated.

2. Communicate about things such as wind direction and whether left-handed players are involved. If the sun is a problem, request that sides be switched midway through the game.

The Essential Communications

1. **Mine or yours.** Yell "mine" or "yours" unless the shot is extremely obvious. This communication is especially useful for third shots and lobs.

2. **Go.** Yell "go" if you wish for your partner to take the third shot.

3. **No.** Yell "no" to your partner if you see a shot going out of bounds.

4. **Bounce it.** Yell "bounce it" if a lob shot may go out of bounds. Usually, the partner who's not fielding a lob has a better view of the ball trajectory and is thus the best person to call out either "it's good" or "bounce it."

5. It's in. Yell "it's in" if you are fairly sure that a lob shot your partner is fielding will land in bounds. (This allows him or her to hit an overhead versus letting the ball bounce.)

6. Switch. Yell "switch" if you are fielding a lob that goes over your partner's head. This means that you and your partner will swap sides, say, from odd-court coverage to even-court coverage and vice versa.

7. Go up. Yell "go up" when a lob draws your opponents back deep in the court. Beginners usually do not move up in response to a deep lob. So help guide him or her by yelling "move up" or "get back."

8. Get back. Yell "get back" when you see that a lob is short, allowing your opponent a smash from the NVZ line.

Many folks are rather introverted, shy, or scared to speak up. Perhaps they are scared of making a bad call. I urge you to get over this and move toward communication leadership. Start small if you must, perhaps by just calling "mine" or "yours" on the service return shot. Then progress to mastering all communications. Obviously, it's much better to over-communicate than to lose a point due to a failure to communicate.

Back to Dinking
Getting into and Holding Your Position at the Line
When dinking, you should try to stay as far forward as possible, in other words, just behind the NVZ line. Your toes should be only an inch or two behind the line. Stay compressed in a basketball-like ready position with your weight toward the balls of your feet and your feet spaced at least shoulder width apart. Be ready to reach across the NVZ line to volley back shots. By staying compressed and reaching across the NVZ line, you can volley back any shots coming toward your feet versus letting your opponent force you backward. If you must step into the kitchen, try to step in with only one foot and then push off with this foot to get back into place quickly.

As crosscourt shots are made, sideways adjustments will be required to stay linked to your partner. The best way to move laterally along the NVZ line is with a sideways shuffle (side-together-side) step. A crossover step places you in a bad footwork position, especially if the next shot comes back quickly.

When your partner is receiving the serve, you should already have at least one foot pinned in position just behind the NVZ line. Once the return shot is made, bring the other foot to the NVZ line if it's not already there. When I play, I set both feet in position just behind the NVZ line before the serve is made. I can still twist my upper body to watch where the serve lands and observe my partner's return. The service receiver's partner should carefully watch where the serve lands and call it "out" as appropriate.

Try to hold both of your feet tight to the NVZ line versus stepping back or moving around unnecessarily. It's risky to look at your feet when you should be looking at the ball. So get your feet set early before net play begins. Your opponent will try to push you back by hitting shots toward your feet. Don't move back. Remember, stay compressed, and volley back shots that are coming toward your feet.

Even though you should seek to keep your toes pinned to the line, twist your upper body to keep your shoulders square to the position of the ball. If your shoulders are parallel to the net and the ball comes to you from the side, you will have a tough time making a good shot.

Practice all of this with a partner or by hitting against a wall. If using a wall, hit with the intention of having the ball land right at your feet. Also, try to have the ball rebound to hit the left-heel target (low to the backhand). So don't make this practice drill easy. Instead, make it tough.

Placement Strategy

The key needs in dinking are 1) keep the ball in play, and 2) keep the ball unattackable. Toward keeping the ball in play, it's a mistake to try to "kiss the tape" or push your shots close to the sidelines. Don't think in terms of trying to hit "winner" dinks; instead think in terms of keeping your dinks in play and unattackable. Toward keeping the ball "unattackable," it's almost always better to hit the ball cross court than to hit the ball to the opponent right in front of you. When you are dinking to the person directly across from you (the near opponent), your dinks have to be about perfect in both height (net clearance) and depth to avoid giving your opponent a volley shot. So the trajectory has to be just about perfect to avoid giving your near opponent an attackable ball. Cross court dinks are more forgiving for both

43

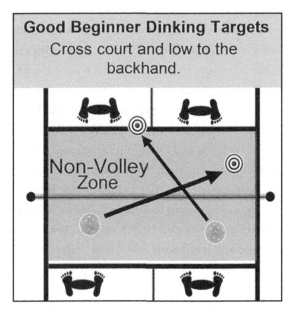

Figure 3-4. A good beginner dinking target

height and depth and they are usually more difficult to attack than dinks that come from straight across. Also, it's a mistake to dink to the forehand of the player right across from you as this provides a setup for a straight-on attack. A good, basic "go-to" strategy is to dink crosscourt to the opponent backhand. About 75 percent of flubbed dink shots that go into the net occur when the player is trying to field a dink that is low and to the backhand.

Let's first talk about shot placement positions.

Key Dinking Targets

Advanced players usually aim at one of the targets shown in figure 3-5. Almost all shots go to these targets only. Basically, you don't hit directly to your opponents. Instead, you hit between them or toward sidelines. Notice that almost all shots require the receiver to reach, move, or scramble.

When You Are in the Even-Court Net Position

Target 1A aims to push the near opponent to the sideline. This target is okay if your opponent is right-handed and a bit too far away from the sideline. Try to get the shot close to the sideline and heel deep. In other words, try to get the ball past this opponent as much as possible. Doing this maximizes

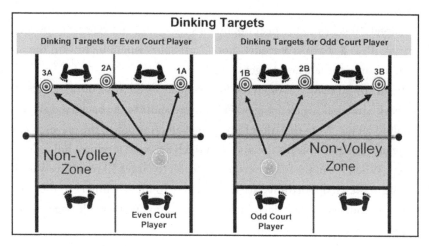

Figure 3-5. Dinking targets

the stress and difficulty of the return, limits the angle of the return shot, and hopefully prevents a sharp crosscourt return. So if you have the gap, penetrate as much as possible, forcing your opponent to play a difficult, low-to-the-backhand shot. If you get a return that is about net high, go for a down-the-middle shot.

Target 2A is low to the opponent backhand and very near the feet. It's rather awkward to return such shots, and you can't do much offensively with these. By continuously aiming just outside the left heel, you can use this shot to push a weak opponent backward. Target 2A also has the virtue that it cuts out your opponent's ability to make sharply angled crosscourt returns.

Target 3A is a sharp crosscourt shot. With a great shot, you can push the far opponent to the far sideline.

When You Are in the Odd-Court Net Position

Target 1B aims to push the near opponent to the sideline. This target is only ideal if your opponent is a little too far away from the sideline and perhaps moving forward. The goal is to get the shot slightly past your opponent. If your opponent is guarding his line properly, don't use this target. Try to get the shot close to the sideline and heel deep. Keep in mind that you are hitting to a forehand and you should not give easy shots to player forehands. So if you don't have a gap, choose another target.

Target 2B is low to the near opponent's backhand and very near the feet. Target 3B is a sharp crosscourt shot. Great shots would be toward the far sideline or to the left-heel target.

In advanced play, you often see long sequences of crosscourt backhand-to-backhand dinking exchanges. Such angled shots to the backhand are difficult to attack. Note that after hitting the ball cross court, the player needs to regain position toward the middle quickly to avoid leaving a hole. Comment: When I'm in the odd court, I usually hit to target 3B repetitively until a hole or attack opportunity arises. Don't try to hit a "winner" to the sideline. Instead, just seek to keep the ball in play and unattackable and wait for a good attack or put away opportunity.

The Virtue of Patience When Dinking

Many players hate dinking for a variety of reasons. Some view it as boring; others see it as stressful. Some folks feel like if it goes on long enough, they will certainly lose the point. As a result, many players quickly get impatient and look for a way out of the dinking game. So they either start a fastball fight or issue a lob shot. These choices, when made due to impatience, usually lead to a higher probability of loss of the rally than would have occurred with continued dinking.

My advice is this: develop your dinking skill to a very high level. It's easy to practice dinking using a wall. Once a dinking game begins, mentally settle in, relax, and resolve you will stick with it until someone faults or a shot with a higher probability of success, such as a smash opportunity, presents itself.

It's great to learn how to steer dink shots, but I would advise against going for "dink winners" such as by trying to hit sidelines.

Defending against Good Dinkers

Now let's talk about defending against opponents who are applying the same dinking pressures. The most important defense is to stay linked to your partner, no matter whether the ball goes to you or your partner. The link can't get broken, and your defensive wall must slide in relation to the position of the ball. When operating correctly, your opponent should not ever be able to hit between you and your partner without one of you hitting the ball.

Thus, always be on the lookout for the down-the-middle shot, which is almost certainly a winner if it goes unanswered. There's no time to hesitate or communicate. So unless it's very clear that your partner has it, if you can reach it, hit it. Better to have two paddles on it than none. Likewise, your team needs to look for and exploit any opponent positioning errors. If the link between your opponents breaks, seize the opportunity by hitting through the gap.

Another thing you must do is stay compressed in the basketball-like ready position. When you are compressed, you can move fast and quickly volley back shots that are directed at your feet. If you are standing straight up (not compressed), you may have difficulty defending against shots that are aimed at your feet. See figure 3-6.

Getting Out of Trouble

No doubt, at some point, your opponent will get you into trouble. A good opponent will try angled shots designed to push you off the court. There are four ways to deal with this type of trouble, depending on the severity of the situation and your skills.

First Choice: If you get drawn out wide beyond a sideline, if possible, return the shot crosscourt to the kitchen, not to the opponent in front of

Figure 3-6. Staying compressed

you. This is called "going post to post." See figure 3-7. Make sure you aim for the kitchen. When in trouble, the kitchen is your friend. A crosscourt shot to the kitchen is your get-out-of-jail-free card. Such a shot should buy you enough time to get back into position. Most beginners, when they are pulled out wide to a sideline, will pop the ball up in front of the near opponent, allowing the opponent an easy put-away shot. So remember, when you get pulled out wide near the net, hit crosscourt into the kitchen if possible.

Second Choice: Only use this choice if you think you can regain your court position before your opponent can hit the ball. If you get drawn out wide beyond a sideline and the ball is too far past you to allow going post to post, drop a soft shot as close to the safe spot (see figure 3-8) as possible, trying to get the ball to land as close to the net as possible. This slows down the game and limits your opponents' options, perhaps allowing you to get back in position.

Third Choice: This choice is the old rule of thumb in tennis. When in big trouble, lob. If you get drawn out wide beyond a sideline and you know you can't get back onto the court in time to assist your teammate, you should lob or try the next choice below, going around the post. Trying to lob while in trouble can be difficult, but it's better than leaving your teammate to cover the entire court.

Fourth Choice: Go around the post. If you have the skill and right setup, this shot could easily be a winner and perhaps a first-choice option. You need to practice this shot in advance via drills so you have the skill and presence of mind to use it when the opportunity presents. To get the maximum width (distance beyond the post) possible, wait until the ball almost bounces a second time (almost hits the ground) before hitting it. Then hit low and into the opponents' court. Note that the ball does not need to travel back over the net, and the return can be well below the height of the net, for example, just barely above the ground.

When the Ball Hits the Net and Then Falls Over
Another time folks get in trouble is when the ball hits the net and then falls over. Such shots are tough to get. A frequent mistake is to pop it up, directing it straight back over the net, allowing your opponent a smash opportu-

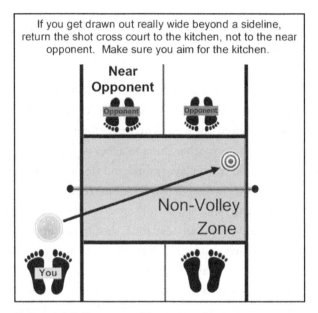

Figure 3-7. When in trouble, return the shot crosscourt and into the kitchen

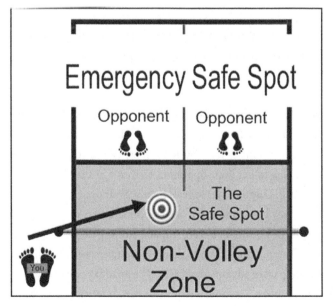

Figure 3-8. The dinking safe spot

nity. Your near opponent will be waiting for this. The best strategy, if possible, is to hit crosscourt and into the kitchen.

Places to Avoid

Now let's talk about where to avoid hitting the ball. Among advanced players, it's not wise to give an easy dink shot to the opponent directly across from you. Especially avoid hitting it to his or her forehand because it sets up a rather easy attack shot. Another thing to avoid is giving the "center forehand," which is the odd court player's forehand (for a right-handed player), an easy shot, as it allows many offensive options. If you watch the pros, you will see that most of their shots go sharply cross court (post to post) or cross court to a backhand. Giving an easy dink shot to the opponent directly across from you also invites a lob. In the dinking game, it's best to continuously stress your opponent, making him or her reach, move, or scramble.

Also, avoid hitting down a sideline twice or more in a row because this may invite a poach of the net from the sideline. This poach of the net from the sideline is called an Erne. Note that the guy this is named after has a name spelling of Erne, not Ernie.

Advanced players can steer the ball accurately, even to very sharp angles. So how does an intermediate player gain this skill? One way is to find a couple of practice partners. Perhaps such practice could occur during a pregame warm-up.

Disguise

When you start playing against advanced players, you will run up against cleverly disguised shots. Learning how to use disguise and deception opens up entirely new possibilities for winning rallies. When you get really good at this, you may be able to get your opponent to move in the wrong direction before you hit the ball. Disguise has several forms. Your opponent may move, look, or posture one way but hit another. Your opponent may make a paddle face angle change at the last moment before impact. Adding disguise to your shots helps shorten your opponent's time to react. Head fakes and misdirection shots are an important part of advanced net play. The head fake involves looking one way but hitting another. To some extent, you can practice this by hitting against a wall. Misdirection shots usually involve angling the paddle so a swing to the left results in a shot to the right and vice versa. These shots may also involve having your eyes directed forward, while the ball veers off at an angle. See figure 3-9.

Another trick is making a sudden change of the paddle face direction via a C-shaped flick swing so that what starts out looking like a shot to the left becomes a shot to the right and vice versa. See figure 3-10.

When playing against these tricksters, you must keep your eyes keenly focused on your opponent's paddle.

Toward developing your ability to disguise shots, you should learn to steer dink shots to the left using both forehand and backhand strokes, and you should learn to steer dink shots to the right using both forehand and backhand strokes. Again, a practice wall is helpful for this.

Lobs from the net and shots to the body should also be disguised by not applying the needed power or direction until the last possible moment. In other words, the shot should appear to be a dink until the last possible moment. If you can't master disguising your shot, at least try to avoid providing a very obvious and lengthy indication of your intent.

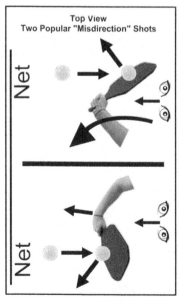

Figure 3-9. Two popular misdirection shots

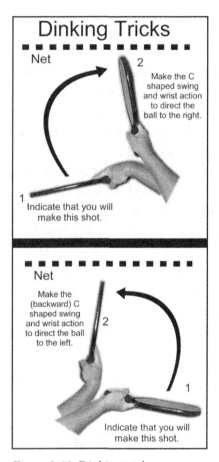

Figure 3-10. Dinking tricks

Capitalizing on Opponent Dinking Faults

The following are some common dinking faults and ways to exploit them:

1. Your far odd-court opponent has a weak backhand and tries to field all dinks with his or her forehand. So he or she runs out wide to field these shots, thus creating a coverage gap. To exploit this weakness, send cross-court shots to keep him or her running out wide. Eventually, an opportunity will present for a down-the-middle shot.

2. Your opponent fails to stay compressed or has trouble with dink volley shots. Many players have trouble taking the ball in the air (taking the ball before the bounce) and sending it back as a volley. Instead, they back up to

allow the ball to bounce. If you can make your opponent back up into no man's land, do it. Just keep hitting shots to his or her left foot. Before long, you'll get the fastball opportunity to allow a put-away shot.

3. Your opponent defensive wall either does not slide or opens up. If you can steer the ball alternately between the left and right kitchen sidelines, you'll put tremendous stress on the opponent linkage. Be patient until the link breaks and your opportunity presents.

4. A dink comes over a little high so you can volley it. Let's say the ball comes over a little high but not high enough to allow a fastball attack. A dink shot that can be volleyed allows making a rather fast crosscourt shot that could outrace your opponent. Also when you get a volley shot and you see a gap between your opponents, this is a great opportunity to go down the middle. If you choose to do this, avoid the frequent beginner mistake of overpowering the down-the-middle shot and going out of bounds.

Stay Engaged

You will often have a situation when lengthy shot exchanges go between your partner and the opponents and you are left out of the action. This might happen if your opponents are trying to exploit a weakness in your partner. During these periods, you must stay focused and engaged. The pros often use paddle tracking to do this. With your paddle up and in front of you, you constantly steer your upper-body frame to track and stay square to the ball when it's in your opponents' court.

Review of Dinking

In golf, putting is often called the game within the game. In pickleball, dinking is not just the game within the game, it's more like the heart of the game. Each team is trying to provide the stress to create a pop-up or hole while their opponents are trying to do the same. The players must be able to both issue and handle the stresses. Dinking skill will determine which team gets the kill shot.

So, practice, practice, practice. Use a wall, perhaps in your basement or garage, to perfect your dinking. Many dinking errors result from mis-hits. Wall practice will help you hit the paddle sweet spot more often. Try to keep both feet pinned to the NVZ line. Keep your upper body square to the position of the ball. Learn to steer the ball alternately left and right both with forehand and backhand strokes. Stay compressed, and learn to make soft volley shots while compressed versus backing up. When practicing with a wall, intentionally create difficult shots, such as making the ball come low to your backhand.

When playing, keep most shots to your opponent's backhand because this will create the highest number of flubs and make aggression more difficult. Stay linked to your partner, and slide the wall in relation to the position of the ball. Use shuffling (side-together-side) steps versus crossing steps when you need to reposition along the NVZ line.

If you get drawn out wide, return the ball sharply crosscourt and into the kitchen. Be patient. If you have a good dinking game and if you can stay patient and stick with the dinking process, this might be your best path to victory. As you get better, try to use methods of disguise and make your opponents move and reach.

Additional Comments

In the previous chapter, I said the outcome of advanced-level play is usually predicted by the success rates of getting to the NVZ line quickly and keeping your opponents away from it. However, teams are often close together on these success rates.

So when they are close together on these skill elements, what's the next most important determinant of winning? The answer is dinking skill. Let's suppose we have two opposing teams, both of which average getting their teams to the NVZ line 75 percent of the time they are serving. In such a case, who's going to win? Answer: the team with the fewest dinking errors. Dinking exchanges, whether at the 4.0 or 5.0 level, usually end by error, usually one of these two:

1. Somebody gets the ball too high, which starts a fast game. This is how most dinking exchanges end, even at the 5.0 skill level.

2. Somebody flubs his or her dink shot into the net, the second most frequent error that ends a dinking exchange. Even at the 5.0 level of play, once

dinking begins, about 25–30 percent of these dinking games will end with somebody hitting the ball into the net.

In advanced play, it's difficult to get a winner with a dink. However, a disguised dink can very often be a winner when used against a player with medium or poor mobility. Many players fail to appreciate the criticality of developing the dinking part of the game. I encourage you to find a place to practice dinking, and I suggest you practice often.

Chapter 3 Quiz

Q1: You are in the odd court, and your near opponent has given you a ball to your backhand about eighteen inches high that you can volley back. The opponent wall is intact and positioned correctly. Where do you hit?

A1: Of course, you could just dink to your near opponent's backhand or toward the T. However, I would use this opportunity to add more stress. I'd hit a sharp crosscourt to the far sideline. As you are catching the ball before the bounce, the redirection is abrupt, and a sharp angle is permitted. Almost any time I can take a low volley instead of a bounce, I'll use the opportunity to try to shift the opponent wall. Of course, you should play within your capability.

Q2: You are in the even court, and your near opponent has put up the ball so you can volley it with your forehand at a height of about twenty-four inches. What should you do?

A2: Because I have a forehand shot, I'll look for a gap between my opponents and shoot for the gap if it's there. This is a borderline case for starting a fast game. I might go for a fast shot to the left of my near opponent, forcing him or her to make a paddle flip, which should give a weak return. A safe shot would be crosscourt and low to the far opponent's backhand. Because the ball can be volleyed, a more stressing dink would be a sharp crosscourt to the far sideline.

Q3: You are in the even court, and your near opponent has sent over a very short dink that makes you step into the kitchen. What do you do?

A3: This could be a setup either for a shot back to you before you can recover both feet outside the kitchen or a crosscourt lob that goes over your left shoulder. So I would avoid returning the shot to the near opponent. Instead, I'd hit to the far opponent's backhand.

Q4: You are dinking, and your opponent's shot hits the top of the net and falls over onto your side right in front of you. What do you do?

A4: Of course, you need to act fast, but the last thing you should do is pop the ball up to the near opponent. Even a low shot to the near opponent is risky because he or she may hit you before you can get reestablished behind the NVZ line. If you have a great touch for lobbing and the ball is not too close to the net, this is a great time to issue a surprise lob. A safe shot would be to go crosscourt and into the kitchen. This buys you time to get reestablished behind the NVZ line.

CHAPTER 4—THE FAST GAME

Now we are going to talk about the strategies that advanced players use in the pickleball fast volley game. Recall that a typical pickleball rally proceeds through four phases:

1. Phase one is the serve, the return of serve, and the capture of the net by the service return team. All these things should happen very reliably. I call phase one the "formality phase," as rallies are usually not won during this phase and nothing very dramatic generally happens during this phase.

2. Phase two is the serving team's struggle to move to the net to achieve equal strategic status with the service return team. This can proceed quickly if a nice third drop shot lands in the kitchen area. Things can get very interesting, and the struggle to get to the net can be tough if the third shot comes in too high.

3. Once all players are fully forward, phase three, a cautious and tense dinking game, begins. Among advanced players who have the ability to keep the ball low, dinking can go on for a long time.

4. Next comes phase four, the exciting part. As soon as somebody lets the ball get a little too high, a fast volley game begins. In advanced play, about half of all rallies will progress to phase four and end with exciting fast volley action. So now we are going to talk about how to handle this phase, the fast volley phase.

Rule #1: Don't Invite Aggression; Instead, Prevent It

About the worst thing you can do is provide an opponent at the net a ball that he or she can volley or smash back at you. So it's important to keep dink shots low and landing in or near the kitchen. Remember, if you get pulled out wide, return the ball sharply crosscourt and into the kitchen. Important rule: never provide your opponent a ball in the air (a ball he or she can volley back) unless it's a shot designed to defeat his or her reaction time or it's a deep lob shot.

Among advanced players, it's not wise to dink to the forehand of the opponent directly across from you because such a shot sets up a rather easy body shot or lob. For the same reason, it's also best to avoid giving an easy forehand shot to the opponent opposite your partner.

Your opponent will also be looking for other invitations, such as a gap between you and your partner or a paddle held too low. So stay tightly linked to your partner, keep your paddle up, and avoid providing your opponent easy forehand shots or shots that can be volleyed back.

Rule #2: Wait for the Ball You Want and the Setup You Want

Most fast games follow a dinking game and commence when the ball gets a little high. The question is when to pull the trigger. Some of this decision should be based on the relative strength of your dinking game versus your fast game and versus the relative strengths of your opponents. For now, let's say all players are equal advanced players and well skilled in all facets of the game. The old rule of thumb is that if you have to hit up on the ball, hit softly, aiming to keep the ball in or near the kitchen area. If you can hit down on the ball, you may hit hard. I suggest sticking to this rule until you can break the rule and, on average, win rallies doing so. You must be careful when issuing a fastball, as you are providing your opponent a ball in the air that can be volleyed back. As will be discussed later, if you start the fast game and you fail to defeat your opponent's reaction time with your first fastball shot, your chance of winning the rally is only about one in three. Defeating reaction time means winning with the first fastball shot or getting a weak return, such as a pop-up, that allows winning the rally with your next shot. So when do you pull the trigger? Let's look at some situations.

In figure 4-1, we see an obvious chance for a winner shot. The ball is high enough to allow hitting down on it. With this angle, the ball is unlikely to go out of bounds. If the shot is aimed midway between the opponents and at foot depth, it will be almost impossible to return.

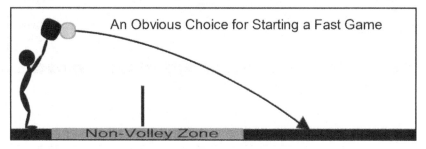

An Obvious Choice for Starting a Fast Game

Non-Volley Zone

Figure 4-1. An obvious choice for starting a fast game

In figure 4-2, we see a borderline case for starting a fast game. The ball is at about net height, so we will have to hit up on the ball slightly. If you can keep your shot rather low to the net, you can hit it fairly hard without it going out of bounds. If the ball is near the center of the court, hit it directly between your opponents. Such a placement will likely cause no return, a weak return, or a pop-up. As will be discussed later, don't hit the ball straight into your opponent's paddle, providing a rather easy return.

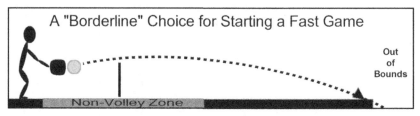

A "Borderline" Choice for Starting a Fast Game

Out of Bounds

Non-Volley Zone

Figure 4-2. A borderline choice for starting a fast game

In figure 4-3, we see a poor choice for starting a fast game. The ball is low and close to the net. If much power is applied, the trajectory will send this out of bounds. About your only hope of success is if you hit your opponent such that he or she blocks the ball from going out of bounds. Beginner players will usually swing at anything they can reach, but an advanced player will likely try to dodge a fastball attempt from this ball position.

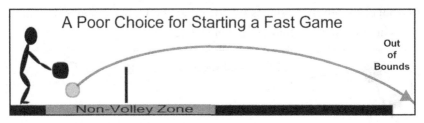

Figure 4-3. A poor choice for starting a fast game

Figure 4-4 shows approximate trajectories of fastball shots.

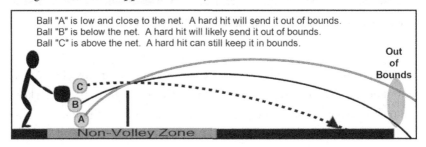

Figure 4-4. Approximate fast shot trajectories

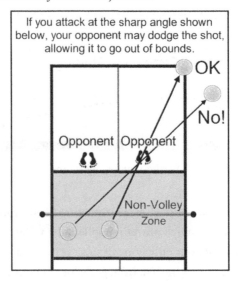

Figure 4-5. Avoid this angle of attack

It's best to have some court behind your opponent. This helps force your opponent to hit the fastball. If you attack at an angle, as shown in figure 4-5, your opponent may dodge the shot, allowing it to go out of bounds.

Rule #3: When You Do Have a High Ball, Seize the Moment

It's good to be conservative, but it's not good to be too conservative. As you develop your skill and play better players, it's increasingly important to capitalize on every opportunity and each opponent misstep. You can't play defensively only and win tournaments. At the advanced level, winner shots, such as successful body shots or shots through a hole in the offense, can often make up 25 percent or more of all rallies won. Even the best players, when they launch a fastball attack, will lose the rally about 30 percent of the time they try. That's OK. In fact, it's great when you win rallies 70 percent of the time. Even a loss rate of 45 percent is OK.

Generally speaking, whenever you have a shot that gives a better-than-even chance that you can shut down a rally with it being in your favor, you should make the shot. Here's why. To play high-percentage pickleball means to play the best alternative with each shot. Most pickleball games are close with the difference between the rallies won and the rallies lost being perhaps a five percent difference. So if you forgo using a fastball shot that has a better than 50 percent chance of shutting down a rally in your favor, you are likely choosing an alternative that will lead you to a 50 percent chance of winning the rally.

Rule #4: You Must Defeat Your Opponent's Reaction Time with Your First Fastball Shot

The statistic is this: among advanced players, if you start the fast game and you fail to defeat your opponent's reaction time with your first shot, your chance of winning the rally is about 28 percent. Defeating reaction time means winning with the first fastball shot or getting a weak return, such as a pop-up, that allows winning the rally with your next shot. If you don't defeat his or her reaction time, you're just giving him or her a nice, close-range volley opportunity. So what this means is, don't issue a fastball unless you are fairly sure you have a good shot, either a hole in the offense or a good chance at defeating reaction time.

If you are successful in defeating your opponent's reaction time with your first fastball shot, you have about a 75-percent chance of winning the rally. So a good first fastball shot gets you an excellent chance of winning a rally. A bad shot gets you a good chance of losing the rally. So how do you defeat reaction time?

When you can't hit down on the ball, you need two main things: disguise of the shot (both the intent and the direction, if possible), and hitting to a hole or location that forces your opponent to take his or her paddle to an awkward position.

Let's talk about disguise. In a fully forward (at the net) surprise attack, you can't just take the paddle way back and drive the ball. A savvy opponent will dodge the shot and let it fly out of bounds. Instead you have to posture and present as if dinking in one direction and then speed up and redirect just before impact.

Figure 4-6. Avoid hitting to the strong hitting position

Let's talk about target location. If you hit to the shaded zone shown in figure 4-6, you are essentially hitting straight into his or her paddle and straight to his or her best place to hit from. Most players can easily hit from this belt buckle position. If your fastball goes straight into your opponent's paddle, you have less than a 30-percent chance of defeating his or her reaction time.

Figure 4-7. Awkward hitting positions

Figure 4-8. Target locations that are tough to handle

Now, if you hit your fastball to a location that forces an awkward hit, you will likely get the winner or the weak return that will lead to the winner shot. So make your opponent reach or take his or her paddle to an awkward position. A popular goal is to "jam" the opponent's dominant side. This means directing the ball to the right hip pocket or right shoulder of a right-handed player. This forces the defender into a high elbow or "chicken wing" arm position usually leading to a weak return or pop-up. See figure 4-7.

Fastball shots that go to the targets shown in figure 4-8 are tough to handle.

Rule #5: When Under Attack, Go Low, Go Near, Go Out, and Go Opposite

One thing you must do during net play is keep your paddle up and angled for making a sudden return. If you have to lift your paddle, you will likely hit the ball into the net. Many opponents will look for the out-of-position paddle and attack if they see it. It's hard to think when you get caught up in a fastball fight. Your reflexive action may be to send the ball straight back to your opponent along the same line that it arrived. Try the following instead:

- **Go low.** As a first priority, angle the shot down, if possible. If you can hit the ground midway between your two opponents, that's great.

- **Go near.** When in a fastball fight—and especially if you are starting it—you should generally fight with the near opponent, that is, the opponent opposite you, not with the far opponent. The near opponent has less time to react.

- **Go out.** Make your opponent reach for the ball. To the extent possible, you need to remember to make your opponent reach out or take his or her paddle to an awkward position. Don't hit directly into your opponent's paddle but go out to either side, forcing a reach-out or paddle flip (such as from backhand to forehand). When receiving a fastball, you don't have time to analyze choices, so going down the middle is usually a great "default" place to go, even if your opponents are well linked. Once the ball is high, going down the middle is often a winner. If it's not, it usually causes a reach-out and weak return.

- **Go opposite.** When returning a fastball or pop-up, send it to the opposite side of your opponent that it came from. As said above, your reflexive action may be to send the ball straight back to your opponent along the same line that it arrived. Usually, this sends the ball right back into his or her paddle, which is not a good place to send the ball. If you get a pop-up or manageable volley shot coming from the middle, you can usually get an easy put-away by going low and to the other side of the same player. If you can force your opponent to flip his or her paddle from, say, backhand to forehand or vice versa, you will likely get a weak return.

Rule #6: Don't Hit Out-Balls

Chapter 9 has more discussion on how to judge shots that may go out of bounds. In the fast game, such judgment is usually required. Fastball rallies usually speed up and get sloppy quickly. In a fast volley exchange, by the third or fourth hit, almost certainly there will be an out-ball. I realize that in a fast exchange, it's hard to do anything other than just react. However, reaction time can be developed via drills, and learning to avoid contacting out-balls is one of the most important things you can do.

Summary

We've now discussed the four phases of competitive-style, at-the-line pickleball. We've talked about the serve, the return of serve, the critical third shot, the keep-them-back fourth shot, the dinking game, and the fast volley game. There's still much more to talk about. In the next chapter, I'm going to move away from strategy for a while and discuss some fundamentals.

Chapter 4 Quiz

Q1: In net play, your near opponent keeps successfully hitting body shots right into your upper torso. How can you defend against this?

A1: When I first started playing the at-the-line style of pickleball against advanced players, I suffered the same consequences. You have to do many things to defend against this. Don't give the opponent opposite you easy forehand shots. Instead, make this opponent reach and move. Watch your opponent's paddle closely. By doing so, you should be able to detect the fastball before the ball is hit. If your opponent tries to get aggressive with a ball that is below the net and inside the kitchen, it will likely fly out of bounds. So dodge these shots. You must keep your paddle up. If the ball is high and you know that a fastball is imminent, preplan to block it down the middle between your opponents. Ultimately, you need to be able to react to fastballs. You can improve your reaction ability by continuously hitting against a practice wall as fast as you can.

CHAPTER 5—PICKLEBALL FUNDAMENTALS

Step #1: Find a Practice Wall or Several Practice Walls

As mentioned earlier, knowing the strategy is only part of what it takes to be a great player. One of the first things you need is ball-striking skill, the ability to consistently get the hit and placement you want. To get anywhere in pickleball, you have to minimize flubs, mis-hits, and shots that go to the wrong place. Players at all levels will benefit much more from practice time than from playing time. This rule applies to almost all sports. While playing is more fun than practicing, playing is a very inefficient way to develop your game.

Here's an example in tennis: For each hour of court time, the average tennis player spends approximately seven minutes actually hitting the ball. The rest of the time is spent chasing balls in between points and getting set up for the next rally. In golf, the efficiency is worse. You'll hit about a hundred shots in a four-hour round of golf. If you practiced instead, you would hit at least ten times more shots.

Poor efficiency isn't the only issue. When playing versus when practicing, you don't get the chance to figure out how to correct your issues or how to perfect shots.

Because it's such a poor use of precious time, professional golfers essentially never play a round outside of their tournament schedule. Instead, they practice, which is a much better use of their time. Coaches involved with aspiring golf and tennis competitors usually specify at least a four-to-one ratio of practice time to playing time.

In the most ideal case, you have a coach, practice partners, a ball machine, a facility, and a schedule. But let's be real. Few people can afford all of the above. A less ideal but still great alternative is a practice wall or backboard.

In pickleball, you'll hit at least ten times more shots per hour using a practice wall (a backboard) than you will hit per hour when you are playing a game. Further, you can learn to steer the ball left and right, and you can learn how to volley, dink, serve, and hit many other shots. You can attach painter's tape to the wall to mark the top of the net location. I realize that many folks reading this will discard this advice without a second thought. Their reaction is the following: it's too boring; there's no time to do this; it's not the same as playing, so it's not going to help; or there's no wall available.

I urge you to not shut down on the recommendation of wall practice. I'll address some of the above issues:

It's too boring: Yes, it would be too boring if all you did was hit the same shot over and over. So you have to practice dink shots, forehand and backhand ground strokes, forehand and backhand volley shots, alternating forehand and backhand volley shots, spin shots, serves, drop shots, and lobs. There are a number of excellent YouTube videos, including some I made that show backboard wall drills for pickleball.

There's no time to do this: As the efficiency factor is so enormous (more than ten times for hits per hour than playing time), you need to spend, say, only fifteen minutes per day doing this to get a huge increase in skill. Because I have a concrete block wall in my garage and a brick exterior to my home, I can easily practice without traveling anywhere.

It's not the same as playing, so it's not going to help: True, you don't get exposed to all game situations, but in a real game, you don't get to repeat shots and focus on specific needs. Practice allows you to take a shot and push it to become better and better.

There's no wall available: I'm lucky. I have a block wall in my garage and a brick exterior on my house. But I also have more practice places. My church has a gymnasium with concrete block walls and so does my fitness club. If the gym is occupied, I hit against the exterior wall of my fitness club. The shopping center down the street from me also has a concrete wall exterior. Some tennis courts near my house have a practice backboard. So I have many places to practice. I think most folks can find one or more places that could serve as a practice wall. You can also practice indoors in your house using a NERF or GAMMA Revolution foam ball.

The benefits that come from using a practice wall will not come overnight. However, if you spend ten minutes per day using a wall to practice dinks, serves, drop shots, volleys, and so forth, I think, within six months, your game will experience a huge transformation. A good player should be able to hit a hundred or more consecutive volley shots against a wall without faulting.

Step #2: Practice the Correct Forehand and Backhand Strokes
Shot by shot, let's look at the strokes that are used.

Of course, the serve is made with an underhand stroke with the head of the paddle below the wrist. Bending your knees will help you make a linear paddle movement through the ball striking zone. I urge anybody who is having trouble with the serve to practice against a gymnasium wall. Use a strip of painter's tape to mark the location of the top of the net. You can also practice on an empty pickleball court.

A standard forehand or backhand ground stroke would typically be used for returning the serve. In pickleball and tennis, the techniques for ground strokes are essentially the same, but there are two differences. First, pickleball strokes need to be shorter and more compact than tennis strokes, because you need to "reset" more quickly. Second, in pickleball, the ball requires more lifting or more of an upward hit than in tennis. For a standard ground stroke, the action is as follows. First, get into position quickly so you don't have to reach to hit the ball. For a right-handed player hitting a forehand shot, the stance will be angled so the left shoulder and left foot lead and are toward the net. For a right-handed player hitting a backhand shot, the angling is opposite. The paddle stays near the player versus being poked out wide to the side. The backswing should occur well in advance of the forward swing. The paddle path goes from low to high and is very linear through the strike zone. When hitting a ground stroke from deep in the court, it's best to wait until the ball is descending before hitting.

Almost all movement comes from torso rotation and the arm hinging at the shoulder. Almost no paddle movement comes from wrist or elbow movement. Movement coming from the shoulder creates a huge radius and thus small paddle path curvature. Through the point of impact, a blocking action is approximated where the paddle movement attempts to follow the same path as the ball for a long distance versus quickly swinging off the ball path. Obviously, small radius swings, as would occur from flipping the wrist or snapping the elbow, require extreme timing precision and thus yield poor consistency. Many unforced errors are due to poor stroke technique. Above all else, think about lifting or scooping the ball from beneath while keeping the swing path rather linear and close to your body. See figures 5-1, 5-2, and 5-3.

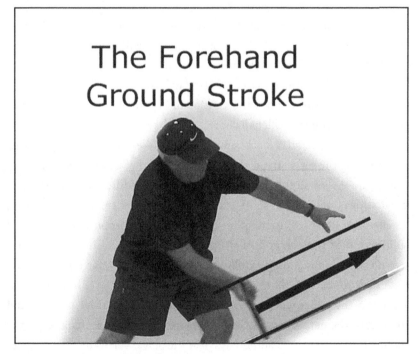

Figure 5-1. The forehand ground stroke

Figure 5-2. The backhand ground stroke

Figure 5-3. Close to your body and scoop the ball

Tennis-like power topspin strokes that attempt to come over the top of the ball usually lead to failure for several reasons: power and control work oppositely, and trying to come over the top is not the correct paddle path. You have to contact the ball below the equator, brushing up, not over.

Many advanced players prefer to add backspin to return-of-serve shots to make their opponents' next shot, the critical third shot, even more difficult than it already is. There's certainly value in making the third shot difficult for your opponent. However, there are some considerations. Can you consistently land the backspin return of serve shots at least halfway back in your opponents' service courts? Can you get to the nonvolley zone (NVZ) line on time when returning serves this way? If you add backspin, don't try to chop downward. Instead, the correct paddle path is near level through the strike.

For the third shot (drop shot), I suggest using the standard ground stroke just described, hitting the ball squarely and lifting from below versus attempting to impart spin. I realize that in tennis, the traditional drop shot stroke goes from high to low (a path shape like a quarter moon) and puts backspin on the ball. Indeed, backspin creates a better ball flight trajectory, tending to float the ball over the net. If you could make such a spin shot reliably, I'd say, do it. However, glancing hits (cut shots) require precision. The third shot is already a tough shot. I'm not in favor of making it tougher via the use of spin. Many coaches suggest using a push shot for making the third shot. The backhand push shot is made by straightening the elbow and pushing the paddle forward through the intended path, with the lower edge of the blade leading to provide lift and some backspin. Note that this stroke uses blocking or linear, not swinging, action. This backhand push shot should be familiar to Ping-Pong players. I often use the backhand push shot for executing third shots. As with the standard ground stroke, when I use the push shot, I prefer to hit the ball as it is descending, and I prefer for the paddle path to be ascending so I'm lifting the ball from beneath. There's also a forehand version of the push shot that also uses blocking action.

For most dink shots, I also suggest using the standard ground stroke, hitting the ball squarely and from below and with most movement coming from the shoulder. I usually add a small amount of backspin on most dink

Figure 5-4. Push shot

shots. As with all shots, you need to bend your knees to get beneath the ball and to help create a more linear paddle path. It's essentially impossible to reduce paddle path curvature when you are standing straight up trying to hit a ball at the level of your knees.

When the fast game breaks out, volley shots will commonly be used, and most of these will use a backhand punch or push. Ultrafast reaction time is required. The best way to build this skill is with backboard practice, making alternating forehand and backhand volley shots. As you get better with the backboard, increase the tempo and distance from the wall. To improve reaction time and fast game focus, try volleying against the wall as fast as you can. With such wall practice, in a short while, your fast volley game will improve dramatically.

Comments

One place I see a good risk versus reward payoff for using a spin shot is with the return-of-serve shot. Your opponents are back, as they must allow the ball to bounce, so you have a large open court to accommodate shot error. A mistake is making a very short return, which can invite aggression. Even for the return-of-serve shot, you should only use the spin shot if you and your partner are committed to being fully to the NVZ line by the time the third shot comes across the net (which you should be), forcing your opponent to make a critical third shot. There's definitely benefit from making the critical third shot as difficult as possible.

A great way to practice spin shot ground strokes is against a wall. I usually practice alternating forehand and backhand spin shot ground strokes. As with the standard ground stroke, almost all paddle movement will come from the shoulder. Rather than the paddle face being perfectly square to the intended ball path, the paddle face will be open slightly at impact with the paddle swing path being out to in to compensate. As your hit is from slightly beneath the ball, the imparted spin will be a combination of backspin and sidespin.

Step #3: Learn the Footwork

1. The Split-Step: The split-step might be easier to understand by watching professional tennis players execute it than by reading an explanation. So if you have access to the Tennis Channel, watch the feet of the service receiver as he or she gets ready to receive the serve. The receiver makes what's called a split-step, a small hop onto split legs. This action loads or slightly compresses the legs, allowing explosive movement. If you watch the top pickleball tournament players, for example, on YouTube, you'll see that they do the same thing. Further, the pros repeat the split-step almost every time their opponent is about to hit the ball. This action keeps you light and allows explosive movement. Pickleball coaches advise that you should split-step every time your opponents touch the ball, which could total a couple of hundred such split-steps per game.

Let's face it. Most pickleball players are over sixty, and many, like me, are experiencing enough pain as it is without such hopping. Even though it's the right thing to do, I simply cannot sustain a couple of hours of playing pickleball if I'm doing a split-step after every touch of the ball. So I cheat. I perform the stop and split-step sequence only when I'm progressing toward the NVZ line.

2. Stop and Split-Step. Starting with the third shot, the serving team needs to make rapid forward progress toward the NVZ line until they can get established there. Unless you are really fast, it's unlikely you'll get to the NVZ line before the fourth shot comes back to you. A mistake is to continue to charge forward as your opponent delivers the fourth shot to you. Instead, you should split-step at the moment your opponent hits the ball and then get compressed. In this stopped-and-compressed position, you can quickly go left or right as necessary, and you can bend forward to volley back shots coming toward your feet. Running forward into a shot headed toward your feet results in getting jammed. Likewise, if you are facing a player who is charging forward, direct the ball so it will bounce just beyond the reach of his or her backhand.

3. When dinking, keep your toes just behind the line, and stay compressed and leaning forward. If you must step into the kitchen, try to step in with only one foot and then push off with this foot to quickly get back into place. Sideways adjustments may be required to stay linked to your partner. The sideways step movement is a side shuffle (approximately a side-together-side footwork sequence). Keep your body square to the ball position. Avoid backing up to field shots directed at your feet. Instead, reach into the kitchen area and volley these shots back.

4. Ideally, a right-hander's forehand ground stroke occurs with the left foot and left shoulder forward. For a backhand ground stroke, the right foot and right shoulder are forward. However, it's not often you have the time to position yourself ideally.

Step #4: Hit Only to the Best Targets

1. The most important target in pickleball is the left-heel target. Remember: left, left, left. In general, for right-handed players, the left-heel target is located left of the left opponent's left heel. So it's slightly left of being centered between your opponents, forcing the even-court opponent to hit a shot that is low to the backhand. See figure 2-8.

Even in the best circumstance when you are stopped, compressed, and leaning forward, a shot to this target is very difficult to return. If you are moving forward, a shot to this target causes a jam or makes you run over the ball. Until a fast volley game begins, this should be a primary target, even when dinking. Recall the other dinking game targets already discussed. This left-heel target is about the only target I aim for when my opponents are in no man's land.

2. Air targets or fast game targets have already been discussed. The most often used of these is the down-the-middle target. This shot often gets through untouched. Even when it gets hit, it usually gets hit with a reach-out, which often leads to a weak return.

Step #5: Keep Your Paddle Up

Among advanced players, most of the hitting occurs at close range. When your paddle is down, you become an easy, vulnerable target for a fastball. In tennis, when waiting for the ball, you should always keep the racquet up and well out in front of you with both hands on the racquet. In pickleball, it's the same thing. When deep in the court, such as when returning a serve, keep the paddle up and in front of you with both hands on the paddle.

When at the NVZ Line

When fully up to the net, keep the paddle up (above your waist) and in front of you with the head of the paddle above your wrist. If the head of your paddle is below your wrist and if a fastball hits the head of the paddle, the impact will deflect the paddle face downward, likely causing the ball to go into the net. If the paddle head is above your wrist, the deflection will send the ball upward, which will likely get the ball back across the net. Some teachers say to keep the paddle blade in a neutral position, with the blade perpendicular to the net. Other teachers advise a slightly or fully backhand paddle position for the at-the-line ready position. I think all teachers agree that once the ball is popped up so a fastball is imminent, the paddle needs to go quickly to a backhand position to best allow a block or punch volley of the incoming fastball. See figure 5-5.

Figure 5-5. Ready positions with paddle up

I don't see most advanced players placing both hands on the paddle when they are fully forward, although I can't see the downside of doing so. Many top players make their backhand backswing using their non-paddle hand as an assist or guide. I think this is a great idea. Your brain knows more precisely where your paddle is located if both hands are on it than if one hand is on it.

Having two hands on the paddle prior to making the backswing for a ground stroke or making the punch in a volley translates into better ball-striking precision. Most strokes in sports are more precisely performed if two hands are used instead of one. For example, you don't need the strength of both arms to putt a golf ball. However, your putting precision is much better with two hands on the putter than with one. If you are shooting baskets with a basketball, you don't need the strength of both arms to make the shot. However, your precision is much better shooting with two hands than with one. When hand painting a sign, sign painters (if they are not using a guide rail) will use two hands, not one.

Chapter 5 Quiz

Q1: My opponents keep sending back their return of serve shots with severe backspin. This makes my third shot attempt nearly impossible. I keep hitting my third shot into the net. What do I do?

A1: Indeed, the third shot is hard enough to manage without having to deal with spin. Here's what you need to do. Wait for the ball to nearly bounce a second time before hitting it. Doing so lessens the impact of the spin. Of course this means you will need to position yourself to allow hitting the ball at this point. In addition, aim a little higher if necessary. Another thing you could try is using a push shot, which adds backspin to your shot. A good way to deal with an incoming ball with backspin is to add your own backspin.

CHAPTER 6—THE USE AND MISUSE OF POWER

You've likely heard that most rallies end not with spectacular winner shots but rather with unforced errors, usually into the net. The main root cause of many of the unforced errors is the use of force exactly opposite of when it should be used. In other words, players hit hard when they should be hitting soft and vice versa. This is especially true of beginning and intermediate players. As with golf, billiards, tennis, and many other sports, in pickleball, power and control are opposites. Hitting the ball harder reduces control and increases errors; hitting the ball softer increases control and reduces errors. Here's why. See figure 6-1.

When you hit the ball hard from the serving line or anywhere deep in the court, the window you must hit through to be successful is very small. A little too low and you are in the net. A little too high and you are out of bounds. When you hit the ball softly, the window you must hit through becomes very wide, and your chances of success increase dramatically. If you wish to explore this more, the angular window of acceptance versus ball speed has been studied extensively for tennis.

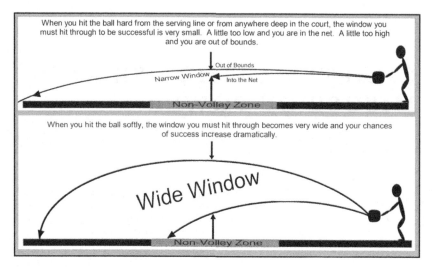

Figure 6-1. The window size

Let's look at specific mistakes.

The Overuse of Power: The Serve

Unless you have extreme consistency with your serve, it makes no sense to use a fast serving speed. To serve deeper, you can hit the ball with a higher trajectory rather than hitting it hard on a flat trajectory. As rallies are rarely won on a serve (among advanced players), for most serious players, it makes more sense to work on serving consistency, not serving speed.

The Overuse of Power: The Return of Serve

The return of serve is where the biggest mistake in the overuse of power occurs. A fastball return, even if successful, rarely gains you anything, and a fastball return will penalize you if you have poor mobility. Using a fastball as a return of serve makes it very difficult for you to get fully to the nonvolley zone (NVZ) line before the third shot comes back. Getting to the NVZ line in time is much more important than making a fastball return of serve. Also, a return that is deep is better than a return that is fast because the deep shot makes the critical third shot more difficult. You'll get better depth accuracy and precision with a slower arcing return than you will with a flat trajectory fastball return.

I think of the return-of-serve shot as a placement shot only. I want to place the ball toward the opponent who has the weaker third shot. Placement shots are most accurate when they are slow and arcing, not when they are overpowered and flat.

A floating backspin return of serve is a great shot if you can execute and place it consistently because it makes the critical third shot more difficult by virtue of the spin. Again, I would not use a spin shot unless you can reliably place the shot in front of the targeted opponent. As you move toward competition-level play, you should never miss a serve or a return of serve, and you should rarely provide a short return of serve that invites a fastball.

The Overuse of Power: The Third Shot
Indeed, among advanced 5.0-rated players, in about 15 percent of third shot cases, the bullet/block/drop strategy is used, and it's only used when the setup is ideal. My studies of videos of hundreds of rallies involving social players find that the bullet third shot is not the best third shot option. Rather, it's one of the worst due to either faulting into the net or going out of bounds. Instead, a medium-speed, down-the-middle shot that bounces before or at your opponent's feet yields the best percentage of favorable rally outcomes. A third shot that bounces before your opponent hits it is a higher percentage shot than a third shot that can be volleyed back or a third shot that has a high fault rate such as a lob or a fastball. (This assumes that all players have equal and intermediate capability.) Remember, in social play, one or both opponents will likely be away from the NVZ line, allowing you to hit a rather easy to execute shot that can bounce before being hit.

The Overuse of Power: Hitting from Deep against Good Net Players
Hard hitters can usually have their way when they are facing weak net players. It's another story if the net players are good. Remember that fastball shots have a small window where they can be over the net but not out of bounds. So a fair fraction will go into the net. Another fair fraction will go out of bounds, and good players know how to judge and avoid hitting these. The remaining fraction of good fastball shots will be dinked, blocked, or

redirected back at your feet. A dink shot is an excellent way to deal with a fastball coming from a player who is deep in the court.

Any time you are not at the net, you should be trying to get there. The best way to make progress toward the net when your opponents are already there is by following after slow shots. So any time you are deep in the court and your opponents are at the net, if you have to hit up on the ball, which is almost always, it's best to target the kitchen with a rather slow, arcing drop shot. The general rule of thumb when facing net players is that when you must hit up on the ball, hit softly. When you can hit down on the ball, as with a smash, you may hit hard. So from the far baseline region of the court, unless the ball is high, you should not be hitting fastballs to the team at the net. Instead, you should be hitting slow, arcing drop shots.

Advanced pickleball players, like advanced volleyball players, understand that you can't win a match by trying to win your points from deep in the court. Getting a winner shot from deep in the court rarely happens. In trying to do so, you throw away the rally attempting low-percentage shots instead of using the rally to create a high-percentage shot.

The Overuse of Power: The Open-Court Put-Away Opportunity

Here's your golden opportunity. Your opponent is in trouble. He or she is off the court wide. He or she has popped up the ball, giving you an easy smash opportunity and a wide-open section of the court. Sadly, with what should be a "gimme," most intermediate players will fault about a third of the time. When you have an open-court situation, don't use more power than necessary to create your unreachable put-away.

The Underuse of Power

OK, we've talked about the overuse of power; where does the underuse of power occur? Most high-power action occurs at the net after somebody lets the ball get too high. When initiating fast net play or responding to it, you must defeat reaction time with your first shot, or you'll likely lose the rally. So never try to start a fastball fight with an underpowered shot. Remember, among advanced players, you should never provide your opponent a ball in the air unless it's either a deep lob shot or a fast shot designed to defeat his or her reaction time.

An extremely valuable skill is being able to keep the ball low and soft, irrespective of how the ball is delivered to you. You can practice this with a partner. Stand at the NVZ line while your practice partner opposite you hits a variety of shots to you. Your goal is to return all shots low and into the kitchen. You can also use a practice wall as follows. Alternately hit the ball very hard and then very soft, ensuring all soft shots are low and over the net.

CHAPTER 7—SHORT/DEEP STRATEGIES

The Lob and Short Shots

Most of the placement strategies discussed so far have dealt more with left to right or horizontal location than with depth location. Now we are going to talk about giving short shots to deep players and giving deep shots or lobs to net players. Some of these were introduced earlier in the book.

When to Lob

Offensive Lobs

The lobs with the best chance of success are well-disguised offensive lobs issued from near the nonvolley zone (NVZ) line against opponents who are also at the NVZ line. An ideal time for this lob shot is when your opponent is moving forward or just stepping out of the kitchen. Here are several strategies for offensive lobs:

1. Feed your opponent a very short dink that draws him or her into the kitchen, followed by a lob over his or her head.

2. Another ideal time for the offensive lob is when the ball hits the net as it comes onto your side. Of course, this will not work if the ball topples over, remaining very close to the net.

3. Here's another time that the offensive lob would be useful. You are deep in the court, and you're hitting to an opponent at the net. Rather than

sending the shot back to you to keep you deep, your opponent dinks the ball instead, forcing you to scramble forward. You're barely able to reach the ball, and your momentum carries you into the kitchen. This is a good time for an offensive lob.

4. You are in the odd court engaged in a dinking exchange. Your opponent hits a sharp crosscourt shot that takes you off the court. A great response would be a sharp crosscourt return into the kitchen. But let's suppose you can't make such a shot. A crosscourt lob to the far back corner (over your near opponent's left shoulder) might be the next-best choice.

5. You are facing a combination of a right-handed player in the even court and a left-handed player in the odd court. So this means that both backhands are in the middle. This is a good arrangement for a down-the-middle lob.

With the offensive lob, the element of surprise is key. So make the shot appear to be a dink until the last moment. The safest ball path is over a right-handed player's left shoulder, over a left-handed player's right shoulder, or down the center line.

I know a few players who have excellent skill with the offensive lob just described. When they issue such lobs against players with moderate to low mobility or against players who cannot smash the ball, they have great success. Indeed, many or most beginner-to-intermediate players handle lobs poorly. My advice to anyone who likes to issue offensive lobs is to try to keep track of your success/failure percentages. If your successes exceed your failures, keep on lobbing.

Many pickleball teachers advise against using offensive lobs, pointing out that the pros rarely use offensive lobs and most other players lose more rallies attempting to use offensive lobs than they win from them. Indeed, most players think they get more successes from their lobs than they really do. I'll also add that it's extremely frustrating to play with a partner who continuously issues bad lobs. My advice is to let the success/failure data drive your choice.

The Defensive Lob

This is usually a shot of last resort. The old saying among tennis players is, "When in deep trouble, lob over the center of the tape." Yes, this applies to pickleball as well. The lob buys you time to get back into position. When in trouble, if you can successfully execute a deep lob, you can go from being in trouble to being in the superior position, especially if your opponent allows the deep lob to bounce before hitting. If you are near the net and in trouble, perhaps drawn out too wide, I'd recommend a sharp crosscourt shot into the kitchen versus a lob.

What to Do after You Hit a Lob

You or your partner has hit a lob shot. What do you do now?

- If the lob is short and your opponent is going to smash it, get back as much as you can, and get compressed and ready.
- If the lob is deep, but your opponent is going to smash it, get as fully forward to the NVZ line as possible.
- If the lob is deep and your opponent is going to allow the shot to bounce, get fully forward to the NVZ line.

Wind Considerations

When playing outdoors, most folks who are experienced with lobbing prefer to lob into a gentle wind. This seems counterintuitive. However, when lobbing, hitting into the wind blunts the trajectory, helps keep the ball in bounds, and provides a nice upside-down U-shaped trajectory that brings the ball down in a near-vertical path. Likewise, most lobbers do not like the trajectory and out-of-bounds risk associated with tailwind lobs. Of course, you should avoid lobbing in strong and gusty wind conditions. See figure 7-1.

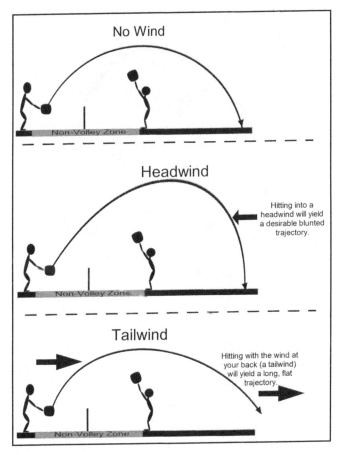

Figure 7-1. Wind considerations when lobbing

How to Handle Offensive Lobs (Lobs from the NVZ Line over Net Players)

The best defense against an offensive lob is vigilance in looking for it. Figure 7-2 shows one of the more frequent directions for an offensive lob among right-handed players. This lob goes over the left shoulder of the left player. Player D should be looking for this lob and then fielding it if it happens.

For most directly over-your-head offensive lobs issued by your near opponent, if you can read it a second in advance, you can take a few quick steps back and jump to reach it. If you can't reach it, it will likely be out of bounds. So it's difficult to lob over your head if you see it coming and react quickly.

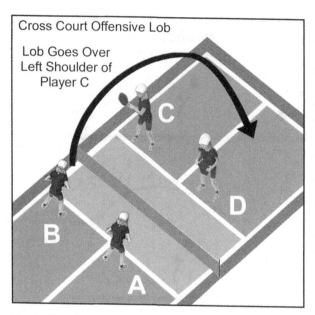

Figure 7-2. Crosscourt offensive lob

Now suppose this lob goes over your head and you can't get it. In general, offensive lobs are handled as shown in figure 7-3. You should get the lobs that go over your partner's head and vice versa. Most social and recreational players cannot run down a lob that has gone over their head. In other words, if they can't get the lob before it passes them, they will not be able to go back to get it. So, in social play, fielding the lob that passes over your partner should become automatic on the part of both playing partners. Quick and reliable communication is essential for every lob. Yell "mine," "yours," "switch," "it's in," or "bounce it" as appropriate.

Of course, when you are fielding a lob, you should try to get into position as quickly as possible to avoid hitting while drifting backward or hitting while running. If you are pretty sure the lob will be in bounds or if your partner yells that it's good, try to play the lob with a smash if possible.

However, if the lob will land close to the line, allow the ball to bounce. After the bounce, try to hit a drop shot into the kitchen, and make as much progress forward as possible.

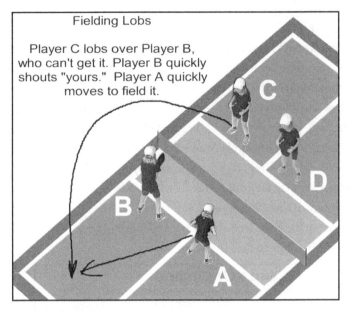

Figure 7-3. Fielding lobs

How to Handle Defensive Lobs

For most defensive lobs and especially for those that come from the opponent baseline, you should have plenty of time to get into position. Your partner should judge the trajectory and either say "bounce it" or "it's good." As
discussed above, if you are pretty sure the lob will be in bounds or if your
partner yells that it's good, play the lob with a smash if possible. However, if
the lob will land close to the line, allow the ball to bounce. After the bounce,
try to hit a drop shot into the kitchen, and make as much progress forward as
possible. Obviously, having the ball bounce just in bounds puts you at a big
disadvantage to your opponents because you will have to begin the journey
to the NVZ line all over again.

What to Do When You Are Deep

You've just received a beautiful, deep, topspin lob shot, and you've been
drawn beyond the baseline about as far as possible. Your opponents are
smartly positioned at the NVZ line. What do you do?

First Choice

From this far back, making a drop shot into the kitchen would be difficult, but this would be my first choice. Make sure to err on the side of too deep (your shot is volleyed back) than not deep enough (into the net). Make sure you follow the shot and make as much forward progress as possible.

In general, partners should play parallel or even with each other. However, this rule does not apply once a player is drawn beyond the baseline, as when fielding a deep lob. If you are drawn beyond the baseline, your partner should get slightly forward of the baseline to field a possible dink back of your lob return shot. See figure 7-4. Of course, if the lob return shot sets up a smash from the NVZ line, the lobber and his or her partner will need to get behind the baseline to field the smash.

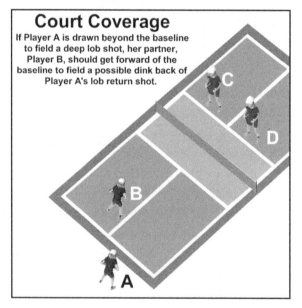

Figure 7-4. Court coverage when one player is very deep

Next Choice

In fielding a deep lob, my next choice for a return shot would be a lob to the center of the nonkitchen area, making sure to err on the side of too shallow rather than too deep (out of bounds). If the lob is too shallow, a smash will occur, so stay back to deal with this. If you do choose to hit a fastball, go crosscourt to give your partner a better chance at fielding a dink back of your shot.

Lobs are a perfect example of how some shots work great in some arenas but not in others. I hardly ever lob when I'm playing 4.5- to 5.0-rated players in an outdoor setting. The opponents are very fast and mobile, and they can smash the ball reliably. In addition, outdoor play offers less control of the ball. However, I use lobs often and with great success in indoor play against less-mobile opponents.

I know several seniors who play indoors who have incredible lobbing skill. In fact, they are so precise that they win almost all their games. So I think lobbing skill is an especially important skill for indoor players. An easy lobbing drill with a partner is to just lob the ball back and forth, trying to get the ball to land in the back half of the service courts.

Short Shots: Three Great Shots to Master

Hitting short shots to fast, highly mobile players who are deep in the court is usually a mistake because you are providing them a quick and easy journey to the net. The general rule is, when they are back, keep them back. However, short shots can work great against your average, not-so-fast opponent.

1. The Overhead Smash Fake (Overhead Dink): The overhead smash fake (overhead dink) is a great shot to master. While it may not work against ultrafast opponents, it will work against most opponents. The shot appears to be a smash until the last moment when you stop your paddle, allowing the ball to bounce off your paddle and fall over the net. Use this shot when both of your opponents are deep in the court, expecting a smash.

Here's an example. Your opponent's third shot came over high. You send it back to his or her left heel with as much power as possible. Your opponent is now in trouble and sends over a weak defensive lob. Both of your opponents are now just behind the baseline, expecting a smash. You set up and pose for making a smash, and then issue the overhead dink. You will likely find that your success rate with this shot will exceed your success rate with a smash.

Many players either can't get a winner from their smash or often put it into the net or out of bounds. You can practice this shot using a tall wall. Direct the ball high up on the wall so it bounces off the wall even higher, providing you a nice fake-smash practice opportunity.

2. Angle Dink of Incoming Fastball: Whenever your opponents are deep and they hit a fastball to you at the NVZ line, a great strategy is to dink the ball or dink it toward the sideline of the deepest opponent. It's difficult to take pace off a shot, but being able to dink back a fastball is an important skill. Practicing with a partner or a ball machine can help you develop this important shot.

3. Angle Dink of an Incoming Third Shot from Deep: Remember, this will only work against an opponent with poor mobility. Let's suppose you made a great semilob return of serve that has landed on or very near the baseline. Your opponent tries to make a third shot (drop shot) into the kitchen, a tough shot from deep. His or her shot comes in just a little high so you can reach into the kitchen and volley it. As you start to hit the ball, your opponent stops and does a split-step. Normally, you would play a keep-them-back shot, aiming for a left-heel target. However, in the situation described, your opponent should be quite far back, as he or she was deep to start with and then stopped because his or her shot could be volleyed. If this opponent has poor mobility, a dink toward his or her sideline (away from his or her partner but not too close to the sideline) might be a winner.

Comment: This is why his or her partner should come forward slightly ahead, and this is why you can't stand still after making a third shot (drop shot). If you watch the pros, they hit the third shot (drop shot) with their body rising into the shot, and then they continue their forward progress. Please note: this does not mean they are hitting on the run. They stop just before they swing and then move up and forward as they hit.

If you can't get a winner with this type of shot, don't try it again against the same opponent, as the goal is to keep him or her back, not give him or her an easy journey to the NVZ line.

Chapter 7 Quiz

Q1: I am getting killed by the offensive lobs issued by my opponents. I don't have the speed to run these down and return them. What do I do?

A1: I know your pain. I've lost many games from not being able to deal with lobs. Here's what you need to do. If it is a third shot lob, don't get to the NVZ line early. Instead, only take your last few steps after you know the third shot will not be a lob. If the lobs are coming from the dinking game, combat them as follows. First, keep your opponents stressed, making them move and reach for every shot. It's hard to issue a good lob when reaching and stressed. You also need to watch your opponent's paddle carefully. You should be able to detect the lob before the ball is hit. Next, you must have an understanding with your partner that he or she will get lobs that go over your head and you will get lobs going over his or her head. This system needs to work quickly and automatically. Of course, yell "switch" or "mine" quickly and as appropriate. It is also a good idea to develop your own lobbing skill. Your opponent may back off lobbing if he or she knows you have better lobbing skill.

CHAPTER 8—THE OVERHEAD SMASH

Here's your dream shot. Your opponent has hit you a high ball that you can smash. This should be an easy winner. However, for 4.0-level and below players, the overhead smash leads directly to a loss of the rally for the smasher about 28 percent of the time. Why? Often, the smasher tries for too much, too much angle, or too much depth. Here's what not to do:

1. Hit it in the net.
2. Hit it too deep (and go out of bounds).
3. Go for too much angle (and hit it out of bounds wide).

Tips for Smash Opportunities
Patience and Avoiding Fault
Here's a common situation. An opponent has given you a smash opportunity. Realizing the mistake, the opponent team retreats to the baseline to field the smash. From the baseline, smashes are not too difficult to field. So the opponent team returns the smash but too high, only to give you another smash opportunity. This can go on and on. Even though the smashing team should clearly have an advantage, too often they lose such a rally by eventually faulting with the smash (into the net or out of bounds). So when caught up in this, stay patient and don't try for too much. Perhaps wait for an opportunity for an angled smash, which should be unreachable. Another great

option after the first smash is to hit a fake smash/dink, if a second smash opportunity follows the first. This should be a winner because your opponents should be deep, expecting another smash.

Where to Aim

When you and your opponents are close to the nonvolley zone (NVZ) line, the best put-away smash strategy is to angle it down to the feet. If you are forward and your opponents are back, your best put-away smash opportunity is to angle the shot to make it unreachable. It helps if the ball is off center because it gives you an even better angle.

Everybody loves a smash opportunity, and it's hard to give one up. However, it's usually best to allow the forehand player all the opportunities he or she can reach. So if your partner is in the odd court and is right-handed, allow him or her to make smash opportunities that are well on your side of the center line. In other words, be generous to the player with the forehand. Communication is key, so call "yours" well in advance to invite him or her over.

The diagrams below show good targets for various situations.

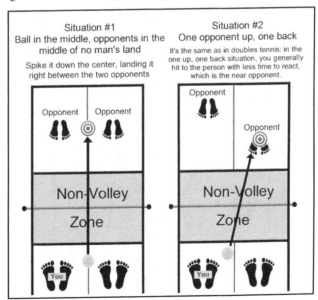

Figure 8-1a. Smash targets, situations 1 and 2

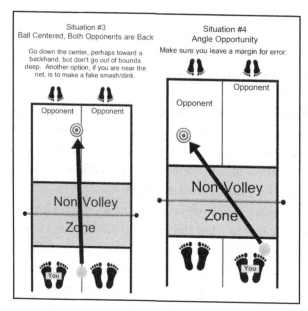

Figure 8-1b. Smash targets, situations 3 and 4

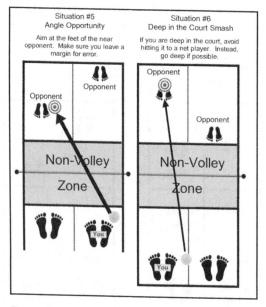

Figure 8-1c. Smash targets, situations 5 and 6

Situation #3 shows the conservative shot, going down the middle. If you are close to the net and are good at smash shots, you could also angle the smash to make it unreachable. In situation #5, it's just like in doubles tennis. Hit to the opponent who has less reaction time, which is the near opponent. In situation #6, you are deep in the court. Remember, when you are deep in the court, avoid hitting to a net player, even with a smash.

An interesting thing about pickleball is that no matter how hard you hit the ball, it's nearly impossible to defeat an opponent's reaction time if he or she is twenty-five to thirty feet away from you. This is why you should come forward any time your opponent is deep, whether he or she is fielding a lob or a smash opportunity. So remember the rule: it's best to hit deep to deep or short (net man) to deep, but you should not hit from deep to short (from deep to a net man) if it can be avoided. You may also hit short to short (net man to net man) when you have a smash because the net man has less time to react.

Fielding Smash Shots

- **Situation #1: All Players Forward:** If all players are forward and you pop up the ball, giving your opponent an easy smash shot at the NVZ line, all you can hope to do is make a quick hop back into a compressed split-step, while holding your paddle low, ready to block a shot to your feet. Note that when the ball is coming to you from below the net, your paddle needs to be held high (above the net). But, when the ball gets high, your paddle needs to be low, ready to dig and scrape up shots that will be aimed low.

- **Situation #2: A Bad Offensive Lob, Midcourt Smash:** In this case, get back as much as you can, and get compressed and ready with your paddle low, ready to dig.

- **Situation #3: A Smash from Deep in the Court:** If a lob is deep, but your opponent is going to smash it, get as fully forward to the NVZ line as possible. If you receive the smash, send it back to the feet of the smasher.

Most right-handed players will smash the ball straight ahead or from right to left, so it's usually best to bias your defensive position accordingly so you are not left of the smasher's straight forward line. See figure 8-2.

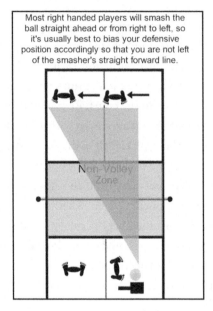

Figure 8-2. Normal smash direction

By the way, a cool misdirection smash to master is a smash with the paddle face open to the right. In this way, a swing path toward the left still effects a ball path to the right. This shot is even more effective if you can add disguise to it.

When you are deep in the court, it's usually difficult to return a smash with a good drop shot. Likely, you will have to return the smash with a defensive lob. Aim this lob down the center line to minimize giving your opponent an angled smash opportunity. Angled smashes are nearly impossible to reach.

Here's another tip: even though an ideal lob is deep, don't aim for deep when you are near the baseline. Instead, aim for the center of the nonkitchen area. Figure 8-3 shows why. When lobbing from deep in the court, you will be lucky to have a pattern as tight as shown in the figure.

The smash/defensive lob sequence can go on for a while. When you are in trouble, your first goal should be to stay in the point versus trying to hit a spectacular shot. Be patient, and you may make a great lob (a deep lob), or your opponent may fault with his or her smash.

If your lob went deep, giving your opponent a deep-in-the-court smash, stay forward and call your partner forward if necessary.

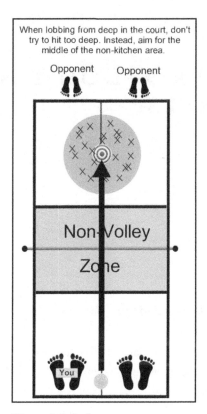

Figure 8-3. Lob target

CHAPTER 9–DON'T HIT OUT-BALLS

How to Judge Balls Headed Out of Bounds

It goes against our basic instinct to get out of the way of a ball headed toward us that is easily reachable, perhaps a ball that's beneath the level of our head. So until trained to do otherwise, most players will usually try to hit all shots they can reach. Consequently, most players will hit many balls that would have landed out of bounds. Among beginners, a "better safe than sorry" or "better not take a chance" attitude prevails. The feeling is that it would be really bad to avoid hitting a ball that then lands in bounds. The problem is that this take-no-chances strategy means that perhaps ten or more balls headed out of bounds were kept in play. Of course, among competitors, every edge is needed, and you can't afford to give away chances to win a rally.

Top competitors are fanatical about not hitting out-balls, and they need to be because so many points are at stake on this issue only. About half of pickleball rallies progress through all four phases, ending with fast volley action. These fastball rallies speed up and get sloppy quickly. By the third or fourth hit, there's a good chance the ball is headed out of bounds. You can't hit these out-balls while your opponents are smartly dodging them and expect to win the match. To transform yourself into becoming a smart player with respect to not hitting out-balls, follow these steps:

Read the speed early. The best way to get an advance notice of whether a fastball is coming is by watching your opponent preparing for his or her hit. A windup (shoulder turn and long backswing) signals a fastball. Whenever I see a windup, I immediately go into out-ball-assessment mode. Good players will try to disguise their fastball plan. Still, watch the paddle speed to get an early indicator of the ball speed. Good players will know the ball speed before the ball is hit.

Know the trajectories that do not work. If your opponent tries a slap shot (a shot to the body) from a low dink bounce or from a dink bounce well inside the kitchen, as soon as you can detect the fastball intent, dodge it. These shots usually go out of bounds. Whenever your opponent tries to get aggressive with a ball that is below the height of the net, there's a good chance the ball will go out of bounds. A midcourt, ground stroke blast will go out of bounds if it's more than about a foot above the net.

Get calibrated. You have to get a feel for the speeds and trajectories that lead to a ball going out of bounds. Start with this rule: when you are at the nonvolley zone (NVZ) line, any fastball coming your way that is shoulder height or higher will likely go out of bounds. So starting out, get out of the way of any fast shot at shoulder height or higher, and watch the results. You'll certainly be right most of the time. Next, lower the maximum allowable height to sternum level and watch the results. For fastballs, you'll still be right most of the time. Of course, both ball speed and trajectory will determine which shots stay in and which do not. The key is to try to get calibrated and improve your ability to judge out-balls.

Live by your calibration. Your calibration may not be perfect, but you must live by it, getting out of the way of all shots you think may go out. You must watch the results. Are most of the dodged shots landing out of bounds? Your goal should be to have judged correctly most of the time but not all of the time. If all the shots you dodged went out of bounds, you are still hitting too many out-balls.

Refine your calibration as necessary. This is difficult to accept, but you must adjust your calibration until some of the shots you are dodging are staying in bounds.

Know where you are on the court. It's not uncommon to see beginners volley back out-balls while standing on or near the baseline. So pay attention to ball speed and height and also where you are located on the court.

By the way, this is a place where a ball machine would be very helpful. From a midcourt machine location, set the ball speed to high and find an angle for the machine that sends balls out eighteen inches out of bounds. Find another angle that sends balls just in bounds. Fire shots from the machine to a person at the NVZ line, alternating between the two angles. The trainee should make quick progress in being able to judge in- and out-balls.

Whereas beginner players will always try to hit rather than take chances, advanced players will more often choose not to hit and accept they will be right most of the time but wrong sometimes. This represents high-percentage play.

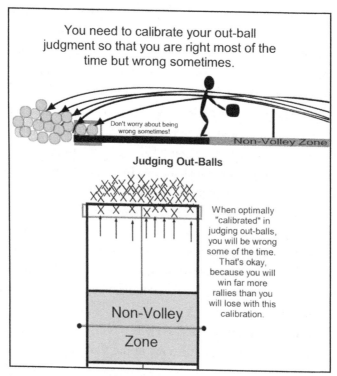

Figure 9-1. Correct out-ball calibration

If you watch professional-level play, for example, the Minto US Open Pro Division Gold Medal Match on YouTube, you will see that the pros dodge shots that end up very close to the baseline, with some staying in bounds. The fact that some shots stayed in bounds doesn't mean they have a problem with this part of their game. Instead, it means this part of their game is likely optimized. See figure 9-1.

Dodging out-balls is also a key strategy when facing bangers, or ultrahard hitters. Many players use hard hits or fastballs as third shots instead of drop shots. Hard hitters will fare well against opponents who save and return their out-balls, but hard hitters will get penalized by opponents who can detect when such shots are headed out of bounds.

CHAPTER 10—DEVELOPING THE THIRD SHOT

The soft drop shot into the kitchen is the third shot that is played more than 75 percent of the time by the top players. If you wish to join the ranks of good players, about the best thing you can do for your game is to learn how to make drop shots into the kitchen. The sooner you learn how to do this, the better off you will be. Not only do you use this drop shot for the third shot, but you also use it whenever you have to hit up on the ball, and you are facing two opponents at the net. The skill level with the third shot (drop shot) is one of the main things that separate the 5.0-, 4.5-, and 4.0-rated players. Recall from earlier in this book, when the serving team makes the third shot of the game (the return of the return of serve) from deep in the court against net players, this shot alone has at least a 17 percent chance of directly causing the loss of the rally for the serving team, usually by the ball going into the net or getting smashed back. The 17 percent statistic comes from an analysis of top 5.0-level players. The statistic jumps to 27 percent for 4.5-level players.

The Best Technique

Before we talk about drills, let's talk about how to set up and hit the ball. One of the keys to shot consistency is having consistency in the setup. There's an analogy in golf with the chip shot. To get distance consistency, you must have a consistent setup, swing, and swing speed, and you have to make good contact with the ball. Here are some pointers:

Make sure you stay behind the baseline until you can judge the depth of the service return shot. A beginner mistake is to advance forward too quickly, requiring backward movement to field a service return shot. It's very difficult to make a good third shot (drop shot) if you are moving backward. Instead, you should have forward momentum into a strike.

Position yourself to maximize forehand hits. Some players can make great third shots using the backhand. In fact, many players prefer to make the shot with their backhand. However, I think most players will get better consistency with forehand hits. So to maximize forehand hits (for a right-handed player), stand left of the center of the box when receiving the return of serve.

Move to the ball quickly so you can have both feet in place and be set correctly before striking the ball. It's difficult to make a good third shot if you are in motion or reaching for the ball.

Hit the ball as it is descending and hit it from beneath, scooping it up. This minimizes the impact of service return backspin and allows using a more consistent paddle angle for all third shots. I realize that with some serve returns, you can't always get into the position you prefer.

Put a good stroke on the ball. Don't poke at it, jab it, or use a wrist flick. Instead, use a backswing, a linear path through the contact zone, and follow-through toward the target, rising forward slightly into the strike. Top players will use this forward momentum to scramble forward after the strike. For forehand third shots, I use a rather linear "blocking" stroke, making sure that the paddle face is aimed upward. For backhand third shots, I usually do the same, aiming the paddle face in advance of the strike.

Partner Drill

You can do this easy drill with a practice partner to help you develop this shot. Start with you and your practice partner dinking back and forth with both of you up to the nonvolley zone (NVZ) line. Slowly move deeper in the court, keeping your practice partner in place at the line. Keep trying to drop

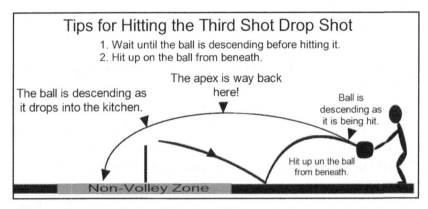

Figure 10-1. Tips for hitting the third shot

your shots into the kitchen as you move farther away from the kitchen and eventually to the baseline. Figure 10-1 shows the arcing trajectory required for perfecting this shot. Notice that the ball descends as it crosses the net. The apex of the trajectory is well in front of the net. Shots that go over a little too high are better than those that go into the net.

Wall Drill

You can use a backboard wall drill to develop this shot. If the wall is not marked to show a net, place a piece of painter's tape at net height to simulate the top of the net tape. Stand about twenty-two feet back from the wall. First, hit the ball rather hard and high at the wall so the return bounce brings the ball back to your location (twenty-two feet from the wall). Next, try to hit the drop shot so the ball descends as it hits the wall. Try to hit the wall one to two feet above the tape. As the ball returns to you, it will bounce two to three times before getting back to your location. After its second or third bounce, again hit the ball rather high and hard at the wall to repeat the pattern. Note, you can practice the drop shot only every other time.

Ball Toss Drill

To get a feel for the speed and trajectory required for the third shot, put away your paddle, stand near the baseline, and use an underhand toss in an attempt to land the ball in the kitchen. Repeat this until you have the feel for the speed and trajectory needed. Now get your paddle, and use a similar trajectory to hit the ball into the kitchen.

As the third shot is so important, much information is available on the Internet, YouTube, and so forth. If you wish to explore this further, use a search phrase such as "pickleball third shot drill."

CHAPTER 11—ONE SIZE DOES NOT FIT ALL

So far in this book, we've talked mainly about how top players play pickle-ball. We've also discussed the strategies that apply to most players. However, some strategies and tactics depend on skills—your skills, your partner's skills, and your opponents' skills. Even the very top players have strengths and weaknesses that should be considered in strategies.

So a difficulty in writing a book about strategy is that strategies often depend on skills and capabilities. Obviously, we can't examine all strength and weakness combinations. So I'll discuss, in general, how strategies can change depending on skill levels and capabilities.

The Obvious

Many player weaknesses such as poor mobility and an inability to reliably hit the ball are so obvious that you don't need a book to explain to you how to exploit such weaknesses.

Examples:

"Just hit it to Joe. He can't return more than two shots in a row without flubbing."

"All you have to do is hit it to Mary's backhand. I guarantee the ball will not come back."

"If Joe comes forward, lob it over his head. He'll just stand there."

"Bob is good. Don't hit it to him."

Much of the advice you read on the Internet is generic, obvious, and applicable to most sports. For example, you hit to the weak player, look for and exploit weaknesses, and so forth. Although simple and obvious, it's still good advice.

Strategies for Most Social Players

Most pickleball players are not 5.0-rated players. Instead, they are social/ recreational players. Most recreational players are senior citizens, some have medium or low mobility, and others are battling at least one orthopedic issue. I can certainly relate to this group of players.

Do the strategies discussed so far apply to this group of players? If not, what advice in particular is applicable to this largest group of pickleball players? This section is intended for social players who are not currently practicing the at-the-line style of play and may never prefer to play at the line.

I have personally taken videos of many hours of recreational pickleball play. I've analyzed the rallies in detail to determine the common faults and assess what does and does not work. Here's what the video analysis of intermediate social play shows. Please note that this refers to intermediate, not beginner, social play. The approximate skill level is about 3.0.

More than half of the rallies are over with five shots or fewer, and this includes the serve. I realize that this sounds unbelievable. Most folks think that rallies last twice this long.

About 70 percent of rallies are over after six shots.

Essentially, no dinking occurs in social play. Instead, shortly or immediately after the return of serve is made, the ball gets high, and the game goes straight into a volley war or fast game.

The first two shots, the serve and return of serve, should essentially be "gimme" shots. This means that most rallies go only three or four shots beyond the return of serve. How do things fall apart so quickly? What choices do people make that lead to failure, and what choices do people make that lead to success? Going shot by shot, let's look at how rallies fail.

The Serve

The service fault rate for the 3.0 skill level is about 3.5 percent. What's the remedy? For the average player at this skill level, the best strategy is to just aim for the middle of the box. Provide enough arc to clear the net easily, and avoid using more power than it takes to hit the target. For most folks at this skill level, it's a mistake to try to win rallies with serves. You can practice the serve without a practice partner. Just take a bucket of balls to the court and start practicing.

The Return of Serve

The failure rate for this shot at the 3.0 skill level is about 8 percent. The most frequent fault is having the ball go into the net. The main root cause behind this is trying to use too much power. What's the remedy? For the average player at this skill level, the best strategy is to aim at or near the center of the nonkitchen area. Provide enough arc to clear the net easily, and avoid using more power than it takes to hit this target. For most folks at this skill level, it's a mistake to try to win rallies with the return of serve. Instead, return the ball slow and high enough to ensure you can get forward and into position before the third shot comes back across the net. Hitting the return of serve cross-court also helps you buy time to get into position to receive the third shot.

The Third Shot

This is where the most vital strategic errors begin to occur. If we remove from consideration the rallies that fail with service faults and return-of-serve faults, about half of the remaining rallies will end within two or three shots following the return of serve. Unless the final shot is a fault, the root cause of the rally failure is usually a shot or two before the final hit.

For example, a rally may go as follows: serve, return of serve, third shot too high, and fourth shot a smash winner. The rally went four shots, but the fault occurred at the third shot.

As another example, a rally may go as follows: serve, return of serve, third shot a lob that is too short, and the fourth shot an attempted smash. In the fifth shot, the smash is returned, but it's a weak pop-up. The sixth shot is a successful smash/put-away shot. Even though the rally went six shots, the key cause of loss of the rally occurred at the third shot (the short lob).

Let's look at how to fix the third shot problem. The third shot will fail directly from faulting (into the net or going out of bounds) at a rate of about 18 percent. Some of these are flubs and mis-hits, but many result from unwise shot choices. The key is to avoid giving your opponent an easy volley opportunity.

About the only thing that separates beginning social players from intermediate ones is that the intermediate people can hit the ball better and more reliably than the beginner players. They have fewer flubs and mis-hits than the beginners.

Strategy-wise, beginner and intermediate social players are about the same. Both groups use essentially one tool, aim for the weak player or an open space. If you ask a social player what third shot strategy he or she uses, you will likely receive a blank stare. Most social players will hit their third shot just like they hit their return-of-serve shot, even though their opponents are likely now more forward. Some players, seeing that their opponents have moved forward, will attempt to lob over or blast through the opponent team. Rarely will a social player slow his or her swing speed to issue a soft shot to their opponents. To do so is certainly counterintuitive. Why give my opponent such an easy-to-return shot? Why not give him or her a fastball instead? The answer, in brief, is that it's better to give your opponents ground-stroke shots than to give them volley shots. Remember the rule: don't give your opponent a ball in the air (a ball he or she can volley back) unless it's a shot designed to defeat reaction time. Giving your opponent a slow ball that will bounce will also buy you time to move fully forward.

Let's look at these four shot choices and the outcomes they are most likely to produce.

Hit the third shot just like a return-of-serve shot. Likely, the opponent team has moved forward. In social play, it's unlikely they are fully forward. Instead, they are likely a couple of feet back from the nonvolley zone (NVZ) line. If the third shot is delivered just like a return-of-serve shot (medium speed that is not too high or low), the opponent team will likely be able to volley the shot back. In other words, they will receive the ball in the air before it bounces, and then they will hit it back, likely aggressively. This usually sets off a volley war or fast game that proceeds through a few hits at the most. Whether in social or advanced play, the first team to provide their opponent an easy volley opportunity gives that team the advantage.

Here's an example. A strategy sequence I often use in social play is as follows. I return the serve to the left opponent's backhand, which means the return is slightly left of the court center line. This assumes that the left opponent is right-handed. As soon as I hit this return-of-serve shot, I get fully forward. The social player, returning the shot with his or her backhand, will often return my shot with a weak and high shot that can be smashed. If everything goes right, the rally is over after four shots. If I can't smash the weak third shot, I'll keep returning the ball to the left-heel target.

Use a lob to go over your opponents. Even when I studied the outcomes of lobs from rather good lobbers, the data still showed that lobbing is not the best choice for a third shot. The better-than-average lobbers had about a third of their lobs leading directly to the loss of the rally. Even social players quickly catch on to the third shot lobber and get positioned to respond to it. I realize there is a small percentage of very exceptional lobbers who will be exceptions to this statistical finding.

Blast through the opponents with a fastball. With speed comes a loss of control. Fastball shots issued from deep in the court have a high probability of going into the net or out of bounds. Even the pros avoid the fastball third shot unless the setup is ideal.

Issue a short soft shot that will bounce before being hit. If you can master this rather easy shot, this is usually the best choice for typical social play. Yes, we are talking about giving your opponent a soft, bouncing, easy-to-return shot. In social play, this soft, short shot is usually not a difficult shot to make. Here's why. In social play, it's rare that your opponents will move fully forward to the NVZ line. Likely, they will be a couple of feet back from it. Moreover, they will likely move forward slowly, not getting into position before you hit the third shot. In addition, it's likely they will not be tightly linked together, and they will not be compressed to field shots that come toward their feet. So if you hit a soft shot, you will not need to hit the rather

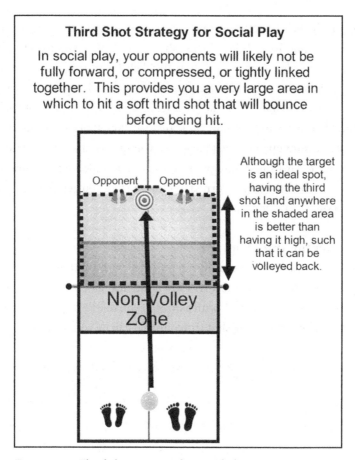

Third Shot Strategy for Social Play

In social play, your opponents will likely not be fully forward, or compressed, or tightly linked together. This provides you a very large area in which to hit a soft third shot that will bounce before being hit.

Opponent   Opponent

Although the target is an ideal spot, having the third shot land anywhere in the shaded area is better than having it high, such that it can be volleyed back.

Non-Volley Zone

Figure 11-1. Third shot strategy for social play

difficult critical third shot that needs to land in the kitchen. Instead, you usually have a large area in which to place the ball. See figure 11-1.

The ideal place to land your shot is at the left-heel target. However, if you miss and go too deep, you'll give your opponent a volley opportunity, which you should avoid. So it's better to land short of your opponent than deep. Don't worry about missing the target. Any shot you hit that bounces before being hit is superior to any of the other three shots described above.

Let me repeat this. An acceptable third shot is any shot that will bounce before being returned. If the ball has bounced, your opponent will have to hit up on the ball to get it over the net. He or she can't get very aggressive with such a shot. In addition, such a shot should allow you to get fully forward. In social play, such a third shot will likely be returned with a shot that can easily be volleyed back. Remember, the team receiving the first easy volley opportunity is handed the advantage. In social play, a soft shot is usually not returned with another soft shot. Instead, soft shots are returned with pop-ups. To sum up, for social players, if you master this shot, it will likely be your best third shot strategy: hit down the middle, soft and low so the ball bounces before being returned. Follow the ball and get to the NVZ line, ready to smash any pop-up.

Shots after the Third Shot

In social play, a soft shot is usually not returned with another soft shot. However, the best strategy is to return a soft bouncing shot in the same fashion. In other words, return a dink with a dink. If you do the opposite—that is, if you return a soft, bouncing shot with one that can be volleyed back—you've given your opponent the advantage. You should seek to keep the ball low and unable to be volleyed back until you receive a put-away opportunity.

In Summary

The strategy just described is really no different from the at-the-line strategy or the approach of the 5.0-rated player. The professional 5.0-rated player will do all of the following, as should any player at any level:

Minimize service faults and return-of-serve faults as a first priority.

With the third shot, avoid faulting or giving the opponent a ball in the air that can be volleyed. Instead, seek to send over a third shot that will bounce before being hit. Follow the soft shot to the NVZ line.

Keep all subsequent shots low and unable to be volleyed back until a put-away opportunity arises.

Shot Placement Choices versus Accuracy and Precision (Capability)

In any sport where you are trying the hit a ball to a certain place, as in golf, tennis, volleyball, or pickleball, to play smart, you must understand your accuracy and precision capability and play within it. So players at all levels need to consider a margin for error or leeway for their shots. The size of the margin depends on your accuracy and precision or capability. Good players usually have better capability than bad players do.

More importantly, good players better understand their capability and play within it than bad players do. In pickleball, even the best players will aim no closer than two feet to a sideline or six feet to the baseline. As with all sports that involve trying to place a ball, getting better involves an ongoing process of reducing variation (which is improving capability), while playing within your current capability. Here are some examples of how placement strategy will depend on server and receiver capability:

- A player frequently faults with his or her serve, going out of bounds deep, wide, or into the net. In such a case, the best strategy is to aim for the middle of the box, keeping the serve slow but high, and arcing to allow a generous clearance of the net. Of course, this player must also work on developing his or her skill, perhaps by practicing using an empty court or a practice wall.

- Another player can consistently place his or her rather fast serve within a four-foot diameter circle. In such a case, this player could pick a target closer to the baseline and the receiver's backhand.

- Another player has trick serves, including short serves, front sideline corner-of-the-box serves, and spin serves. These trick serves, although often faulting, yield far more winners than faults when used against novices and folks with poor mobility. However, these trick serves yield more faults than winners when used against skilled players. So such serves are high-percentage shots when the receiver has low capability but are low-percentage shots when the receiver has high capability.

As you can see, there's not a one-size-fits-all answer to how you should serve the ball or return a serve. A fast player can follow his or her fast return. A slow player must return a serve with a slow shot to enable getting to the NVZ line before the third shot comes back.

Player Mobility and Speed
Lobs

Much argument goes on in the pickleball world about whether lobs should be used or not. Some folks argue, because the top 5.0-rated players rarely lob, the rest of us should not do it either. Playing smart means picking the highest percentage shot among the options available to you. If your opponents are not fully forward, lobbing is likely not the highest percentage option. If you are deep in the court, lobbing is likely not your highest percentage option. When you are in trouble, lobbing may be the only option with any chance of success. A key consideration with the lob is the capability of the lobber and those receiving the shot. Lobs can be a high-percentage shot if the lobber has good capability and if his or her opponents have poor or average capability in handling them. And the reverse is true. Lobs are a low-percentage shot if the lobber has poor capability and his or her opponents have good capability in handling them.

So lobs are a perfect example of how some shots work great in some arenas but not others. I hardly ever lob when I'm playing 4.5- to 5.0-rated players in an outdoor setting. The opponents are very fast and mobile, and they can smash the ball reliably. In addition, outdoor play offers less control of the ball. However, I use lobs with great success in indoor play against less-mobile opponents.

As most players are at or below the 4.0 level, I think developing lobbing skill is important, especially for indoor players. An easy lobbing drill with a partner is to just lob the ball back and forth, trying to get the ball to land in the back half of the service courts.

Short Shots

Hitting short shots to fast, highly mobile players who are deep in the court is usually a mistake because you are providing them a quick and easy journey to the net. The general rule is, when they are back, keep them back. However, the overhead fake smash/dink and dink back of shots that come from deep in the court can be high-percentage winner shots when used against folks with average or low mobility.

Conclusions

Some strategies and tactics depend on skills—yours, your partner's, and your opponents'. When employing trick serves, lobs, short shots, or any risky shot, it's important to track and understand your real percentages.

What to Do If You Have Poor Mobility

Currently, most pickleball players are over sixty years old, and a majority have medium or rather poor mobility. I'm in this situation. If a well-disguised offensive lob issued from the NVZ line comes directly over my head, I usually have to yell "yours." If you have medium or poor mobility but are otherwise comfortable with at-the-line play, here's what you have to remember:

- When you are on the serving team, stay behind the baseline until you can judge where the return shot will land. Low-mobility players should avoid retreating and trying to run backward.
- After returning the serve, get fully to the NVZ line on time before the third shot comes across the net. If you are rather slow like I am, you will likely need to return the serve with an arcing semilob to provide you enough time to be fully forward. Low mobility is less of an issue at the NVZ line than it is when deep in the court.
- If you are playing at-the-line opponents, you have to learn how to make the third shot drop shot into the kitchen. One of the worst things a low-mobility player can do when he or she is deep in the court is hit a fastball shot to a net player who can dink it. You will never reach the dink.
- The worst threat the low-mobility player has to face when at the NVZ line is the sneaky offensive lob. To deal with this, you need to tell your partner in advance to field all lobs going over your head and yell "yours" when they happen. In addition, you need to learn how to make these sneaky lobs yourself. I know a low-mobility player in his seventies who consistently (and successfully) issues the offensive lob almost immediately after the dinking game begins. His strategy is to get them before they get him. In his case, this strategy works

well because he has mastered the shot and is not playing level 4.0 and higher players.

- When you and your partner are deep in the court, your higher mobility partner may need to cover a good portion of your territory. This keeps the low-mobility player from getting pinned near the baseline.
- If you are engaged in tournament play, you should seek a partner who can field lobs that go over your head. A poor tournament partnership arrangement is one where both partners have poor mobility. In addition, you may need to consider stacking.
- When you have low mobility, strive to get the rest of your game to the highest level possible to make up for the low-mobility issue. I know many folks who have done this.

What to Do When Your Opponent Has Poor Mobility

Throughout this book, I have discussed strategies to use with low-mobility players, and these strategies work well in social play. In particular, Chapter 7 on short/deep strategies has great information. In social play, I usually do not use offensive lobs against opponents with handicaps.

CHAPTER 12—HOW TO HANDLE THE POWER PLAYER

"Beating Bangers"

Hard-hitting bangers usually do OK among midlevel players for many reasons. Midlevel players are often not at the net when they should be. This means the fastball can attack the feet. Midlevel players also don't know what to do with an incoming fastball (like dinking it or blocking it to the backhand). Midlevel players can't judge and thus return out-balls. Further, many midlevel players simply can't handle the speed and thus flub the return of the fastball. So here's how to handle hard-hitting opponents.

When You Serve

If you have the skill to do it reliably, try to serve to the banger's backhand, as this should create a weaker return of the serve. Further, whenever hitting to the banger, try to keep most or all shots to the banger's backhand.

When You Return Serve

You are facing your opponent banger who has a very fast serve. Make sure you are standing well behind the baseline, and wait for the ball to descend before hitting it. There is no need for your return-of-serve shot to be fast, but it's helpful if it's deep. Let's assume you are facing two bangers who will both hit fastball third shots. Either hit to the weaker banger or to the left-heel target of the banger in the even court.

When You Are Fielding the Third Shot

When playing against bangers, it's even more critical to get fully to the non-volley zone (NVZ) line on time to receive the third shot. If you are slow getting forward, you are inviting a fastball shot to stop your progress. So you are at the NVZ line, and the banger is blasting a shot at you. This is a situation where it's really important to be able to judge and not hit out-balls. A high percentage of fastball third shots will go out of bounds.

If the banger is deep (near or beyond the baseline), dink the fastball shot. By the way, all players need to learn how to dink back incoming fastball shots. As a last resort, just block the shot toward the left-heel target, seeking to stop forward progress. Remember, when they are back, keep them back.

The Fourth Shot and Beyond

Again, when hitting to a banger, try to keep most or all shots to the banger's backhand and to the left-heel target. Whenever your opponent tries to get aggressive with a ball that is below the height of the net, there's a high probability that the shot will go out of bounds.

Drills

To be a good pickleball player, you have to be able to handle fastballs. A practice partner can help you with this. Stand at the NVZ line, and start with having the fastball come to you from deep. Learn to block the fastball toward the sender's feet and to dink it into the kitchen and toward a sideline. As you get better, have the fastballs come to you from a closer distance.

A great way to build reflexes and the ability to handle fast shots is by hitting volley shots against a backboard. Practice continuous volleying without letting the ball bounce. As you improve, increase your hitting speed and distance from the wall.

CHAPTER 13—SHOTS TO AVOID

Almost all pickleball players underestimate how difficult it is to hit a target spot on the court. The consequence is that too little margin for error is allowed, resulting in shots going out of bounds. To better convince yourself of the difficulty of ball placement, try this test. Try to return all serves for an entire game to the target location shown in figure 13-1, which should force a backhand return for a right-handed player. Now how did you do? Almost certainly, your pattern was no better than that shown below.

With these results in mind, you should be convinced that some shots should be avoided. Here are some shots to avoid.

Going Down the Sideline When You Are Deep

You are deep in the court, and your near opponent at the nonvolley zone (NVZ) line appears to have left the sideline alley unprotected. What a joy it would be to burn this guy and smoke a fastball down the sideline! Indeed, when you are successful in making such a shot, it brings tremendous pride. It's like sinking a jump shot from twenty-five feet. Following the no-guts-no-glory credo, you go for it. Unfortunately, your shot goes wide. Was the miss a fluke?

No. Every book on doubles tennis strategy lists the down-the-alley passing shot as a low-percentage shot to avoid. It's the same in pickleball. See

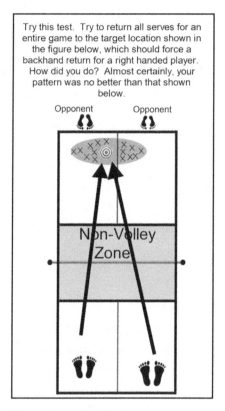

Figure 13-1. Try this test

figure 13-2. Such a shot has a high risk of either getting picked off by the near net player or going out of bounds wide. Rarely will you see a 5.0-rated player attempt such a down-the-sideline shot. A better choice is to focus on getting yourself to the net by placing a drop shot into the kitchen. I agree with what one coach told me: only go down the sideline if the hole is big enough to drive a truck through.

Hitting down the sideline from the NVZ line or close to the NVZ line can be a great shot if your near opponent is too far to the center, especially if he or she is running forward as well. Also, when you are at the NVZ line, if a volley opportunity presents itself, this can be a good time to go down the line, especially if the shot creates a reach-out or a paddle flip, say, from backhand to forehand.

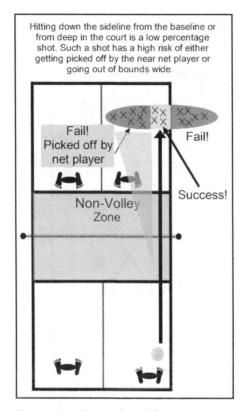

Figure 13-2. Down the sideline

Long Crosscourt Shots toward a Sideline

Hitting diagonally toward a kitchen sideline from the NVZ line, as when dinking, is OK. Indeed, just like in doubles tennis, clearing the middle for a down-the-center winner is a great strategy. Hitting a crosscourt drop shot designed to land in the kitchen is also OK. However, a long crosscourt shot toward a sideline issued from the baseline or from deep in the court is a low-percentage shot. See figure 13-3. Again, books on doubles tennis strategy advise against these shots as they so often result in going out of bounds. Rarely will you see a top-rated player attempt such a long diagonal shot.

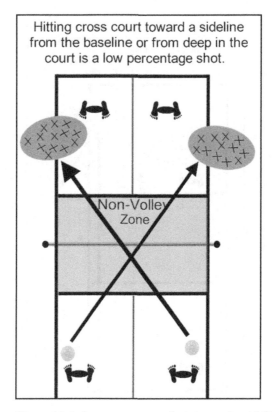

Figure 13-3. Long crosscourt shots toward a sideline

Lobbing from the Baseline or from Deep in the Court

When you are in trouble, such as when a net man is smashing a ball at you, lobbing from the baseline is OK. However, lobbing from the baseline when you are not in trouble is usually a poor strategy. Especially as a third shot, it's tempting to go over the heads of the team at the net. Sneaky lobs while dinking are effective, but to lob from the baseline or from deep in the court is a low-percentage shot as your opponents have plenty of time to react and move. If you are good at lobbing, you might fare OK against players with poor mobility or those who botch their smash shots. However, against good players, for every point gained from this, you will likely lose two. If you are not great at lobbing, you will hit half of your lobs too short, resulting in a smash, and you'll hit half too long, resulting in out of bounds. A better

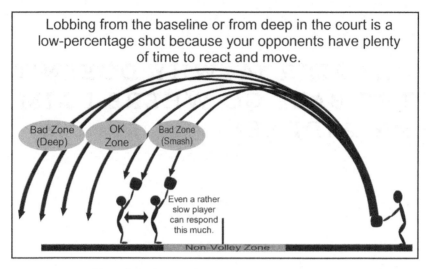

Lobbing from the baseline or from deep in the court is a low-percentage shot because your opponents have plenty of time to react and move.

Bad Zone (Deep)   OK Zone   Bad Zone (Smash)

Even a rather slow player can respond this much.

Non-Volley Zone

Figure 13-4. Lobbing from deep in the court

choice is to focus on getting yourself to the net by means of following a soft shot intended to drop into the no volley zone.

Topspin Fastball Shots from Deep in the Court

Unlike in tennis, fastball ground-stroke shots are rarely needed in doubles pickleball. However, such a shot is used for making the third shot drive and in the unusual case of a deep player hitting to another deep player. Among mid-level players, fastball shots issued from deep in the court have about a twenty five percent direct failure rate, either going into the net or going out of bounds deep. Adding topspin adds to the difficulty of making the shot. Unlike in table tennis, you can't add topspin by coming over the top of the ball. Instead, you have to add lift, contacting the ball below the center as the paddle brushes upward.

Comments

Most low-percentage shots come from impatience, desperation, or the beginner desire to win the point with every shot taken. You simply cannot go for a winner with every shot you take. Instead, you have to patiently wait for an opportunity or set up circumstances that can create winning opportunities.

CHAPTER 14—WHY DOESN'T THE BALL GO WHERE I AIM MY PADDLE?

Almost all pickleball players underestimate how difficult it is to hit a target spot on the court. Most people think the ball should travel in the direction where they aim their paddle. But usually, the ball does not. Yes, a frustrating fact is that the ball usually does not travel along the path of the strike. In other words, the ball does not go where the paddle is aimed.

Let's look at a simple case. A shot is coming from crosscourt, and you wish to simply block it straight forward. So you aim your paddle straight forward. Does the ball go forward, perpendicular to the face of your paddle? No. Instead, it leaves that paddle at about the same angle it came in from. In physics, it's called the law of reflection. See figure 14-1.

Here's a similar case. You are fully forward at the NVZ line, and your very deep opponent hits a fastball to you. You wish to dink it (block it) toward a sideline. In such a case, you can't aim the paddle directly at the target. Instead, you must aim it slightly toward the direction the ball is coming from.

To make matters worse, ball spin can increase the angle of reflection even more so that the ball comes off the paddle at an angle nowhere near where you are aiming it. See figure 14-2.

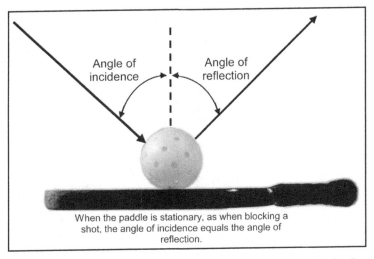

Figure 14-1. Blocking shot/angle of incidence equals the angle of reflection

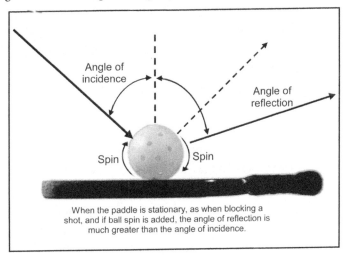

Figure 14-2. Effect of spin

Now let's look at the normal case. A shot is coming to you from some angle, and you are aiming your paddle at a target and striking the ball. Will the ball hit the target? Almost certainly not. The forward motion of the paddle reduces but does not eliminate the angle of reflection. See figure 14-3.

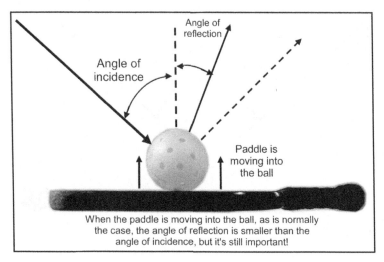

Figure 14-3. When the paddle is moving

The faster the paddle moves into the ball, the smaller the angle of reflection will be. In other words, with a fast hit, the ball will come off the paddle more closely to the direction the paddle is aimed.

Please don't interpret this to mean that hitting harder is better. Remember that the vertical window of acceptance becomes smaller as power is increased.

So what are the takeaways from this? Here are the key points:

1. If a return does not change the ball angle, in other words, if the ball is sent back along the same direction it arrived, it will be easier to control the direction of the ball. In such a case, the ball's incoming and outgoing directions are the same and perpendicular to the face of the paddle at contact. Thus, the angle of incidence and the angle of reflection are both zero. Unless there is spin on the ball, the ball will go out in the direction of the paddle path, whether the player swings hard, softly, or somewhere in between. Such shots, although easy to control, are not always a great choice.

2. Be careful when trying to change the direction of the ball. When you change the direction of the ball, you must compensate for the angle of reflection. You do this as follows. If the ball is coming to you from the crosscourt direction and you wish to send the ball straight forward, perpendicular to

the net, you will need for your swing path and paddle face to be slightly crosscourt, that is, slightly toward the direction the ball is coming from. The amount of compensation will depend on how hard you are hitting. You can't play great pickleball without learning how to change the direction of the ball. A great wall practice drill is to get in a corner and alternately hit to each wall.

3. Allow for error. The farther back you are from the net, the more important it becomes to stay away from sidelines. Aside from the angle of reflection problem is the problem of spin. It's hard to judge the direction and level of ball spin. If you are at your baseline and there is no spin and no intended ball direction change, a paddle face error of only five degrees translates into being laterally off-target by about four feet at your opponent's end of the court. So allow for error!

Here are some common mistakes.

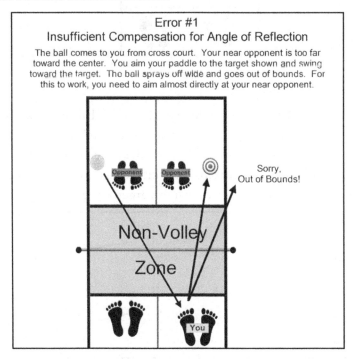

Figure 14-4. Insufficient compensation

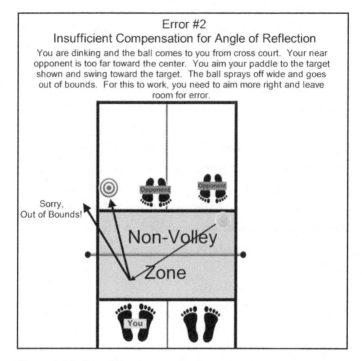

Figure 14-5. Insufficient compensation

Whenever you are changing the direction of the ball and attempting to make a rather soft shot such as a dink, the angle of reflection will be large, and you can easily go out of bounds wide. This is a common beginner mistake. It's much easier and safer to take a soft shot and change its direction to a longer and faster shot than the other way around. See figure 14-6.

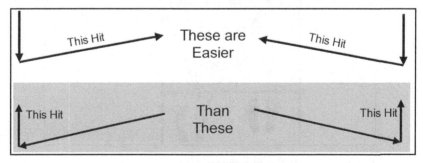

Figure 14-6. Short soft shots require less skill to redirect

CHAPTER 15—MISCELLANEOUS SHOTS AND SITUATIONS

In this chapter, I'm going to talk about special and unusual situations.

High Bounce Near the Net: Either Dink or Go Sharp Diagonal

A high, defensive lob is really short. It looks like it may not make it over the net, but it does. How do you handle this? Of course, because it's in the kitchen, you can't hit it until after the bounce. After the bounce, the ball will be about thirty-six inches high. If your opponents are about ten feet or more away from the ball, a tiny, disguised dink to put the ball just barely back across the net should be a winner.

But let's say your opponents are fully forward. If the ball comes up higher than the net, you could go for a body shot to the near opponent. However, because the ball is close to the net and will likely come up slightly above it, I would likely choose to hit a sharply angled (and fairly sharply down) shot to send the ball sharply crosscourt and very wide.

If the high shot seems sure to come across the net and if it's close to a sideline, you could try the Erne shot described below.

Around the Post

You are dinking, and a sharply angled shot pulls you out wide, outside of the court. Only your partner is left to cover the whole court. The worst thing to do is to hit the ball to the near opponent. A better idea is to go sharply cross-court and into the kitchen. However, if the ball is really wide, the around-the-post shot gives you the best chance for a winner. You need to practice this shot via drills in advance of use so you have the skill and presence of mind to use it when the opportunity presents. To get the maximum width (distance beyond the post) possible, wait until the ball almost bounces a second time (almost hits the ground) before hitting it. Then hit low and into the opponents' court. Note that the ball does not need to travel back over the net. And the return can be well below the height of the net, for example, just barely above the ground.

The Erne Shot, Smashing from Out of Bounds on the Side

You are dinking back and forth with your opponent along a sideline. You see that he or she is going to continue to go down the sideline. You may move to the side of the court (outside the court) and near the net and post to smash the ball as it comes across the net. Most players try to avoid stepping into the kitchen when moving to the side area. If you touch the nonvolley zone (NVZ) for any reason, you cannot volley the return until both feet have made contact with the playing surface completely outside the NVZ.

Your paddle can break the plane of the net on the follow-through but not touch the net. You may also go around the net post and cross the imaginary extension of the net so long as you do not touch the opponent's court. You can sometimes bait your opponent to hit it to you down the sideline to set up the Erne shot. If your opponent is slightly too far to the center where you can get the ball past him or her down the sideline, he or she can likely return the ball only forward, not crosscourt. You can also use the Erne outside of the dinking game, such as if an opponent hits a third shot (drop shot) that is too close to a sideline or if a short lob comes near a sideline.

Player in the Kitchen

Your shot hits the top of the net but dribbles over the net into your near opponent's kitchen area. He or she gets the ball back over the net to you and struggles to get out of the kitchen. What do you do? Unless he or she is ultrafast in getting back behind the NVZ line, send the ball back to him or her, attempting to make a body shot.

Once your opponent steps both feet into the kitchen, he or she must get both feet back on the ground outside of the kitchen (behind the NVZ line) before he or she can make a volley shot. This is tough to do. Note that this is also why, when it happens to you, you need to return the shot crosscourt to give yourself time to get back behind the line (and to make a body shot attempt more difficult). Remember also that you should not put both feet into the kitchen unless it can't be avoided.

Open Net Position/Poach and Fake Poach

A great crosscourt dink to a sideline drew your teammate off the court and he or she can't recover in time to field the next shot. Unfortunately, he or she did not lob but hit the ball to his or her near opponent. So his or her net position is open and this leaves you trying to defend the entire court. What do you do? This is a very difficult situation to handle. The worst thing to do is stay in place, guarding your part of the court. A slightly better choice is to move to the center of the court. This still leaves room for a passing shot through your teammate's vacant side of the court. To properly bisect your opponent's angle of opportunity, you must move into your teammate's vacant court, at least slightly. The opponent will be predisposed to hit in this direction rather than sharply crosscourt. Another option when you have an open net position is to do a fake poach. The fake poach might draw the shot right to you.

The Keep-Them-Back Shot That Can Be Volleyed

Your third shot (drop shot) landed in the kitchen, and you are proceeding forward to the NVZ line. You are still five or six feet from the NVZ line when the keep-them-back shot comes to you. This shot comes to your forehand and is low but can be volleyed. What do you do? A conservative shot would be to play a drop shot into the kitchen and proceed toward the NVZ line. However, this could be a good time to hit a fastball to the soft center (the center point between your two opponents), which often causes a weak or popped-up return.

The Semi-Smash Angled Put-Away Shot (Figure 15-1)

You receive a ball in the air (one that can be volleyed) that's slightly above the height of the net. Your opponents are not yet fully forward. What do you do? Of course, you could play a keep-them-back shot aiming for a left-heel target. However, you can likely get a winner if you hit sharply crosscourt using as much pace as possible. This should make the ball unreachable.

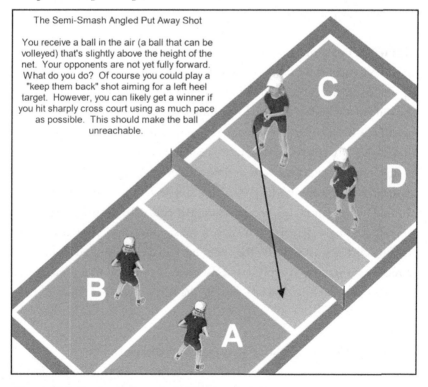

Figure 15-1. Semi-smash angled put-away shot

Low-Mobility Player Hits Third Shot from Back T, Gets Pinned to Baseline (Figure 15-2)

The return of serve goes deep and to the backhand of low mobility player A who is in the deuce (even) court. He or she tries to make a soft third drop shot into the kitchen, but the shot is slightly high and can be volleyed back. The net player C dinks it away from player A for a winner. Even if the third shot went to net player D, the same winner play can be made.

Comment: Player B instead of player A should field return of serves that come within a few feet of the center line. So player B should yell "mine." This keeps the low-mobility player from getting pinned to the baseline. Also, forehand third shots are usually better than backhand third shots.

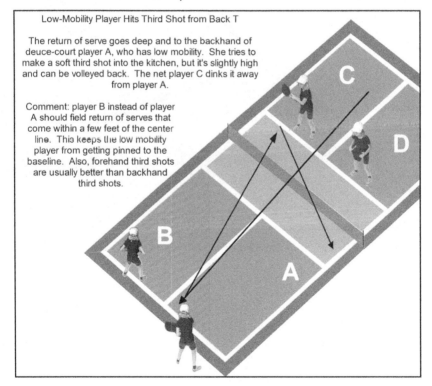

Low-Mobility Player Hits Third Shot from Back T

The return of serve goes deep and to the backhand of deuce-court player A, who has low mobility. She tries to make a soft third shot into the kitchen, but it's slightly high and can be volleyed back. The net player C dinks it away from player A.

Comment: player B instead of player A should field return of serves that come within a few feet of the center line. This keeps the low mobility player from getting pinned to the baseline. Also, forehand third shots are usually better than backhand third shots.

Figure 15-2. Low-mobility player gets pinned to baseline

Defeat the Defensive Wall (Figure 15-3)

When dinking, the defensive wall has plenty of time to slide back and forth so long as the ball bounces between hits. If you receive a shot near a sideline that can be volleyed, a sharp crosscourt dink might be able to outrace your far opponent for a winner or weak return.

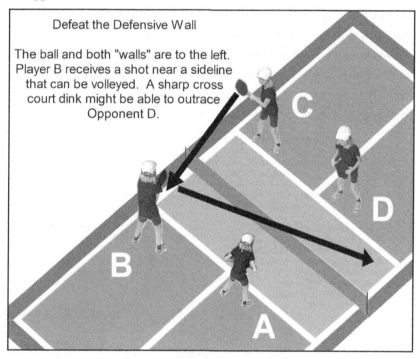

Figure 15-3. Defeat the defensive wall

CHAPTER 16—THE WINNING PHILOSOPHY

As we've already discussed, to win at pickleball, you must have skills, mobility, and strategy. You need to have ball-striking and shot-making skills, the ability to move quickly to field shots, and a thorough understanding of strategy—where to be and where to hit the ball for every situation.

I believe another element separates the best from the rest: it's how you think. Many top players in a variety of sports such as golf, tennis, soccer, and basketball will even say that what separates the very best from the very good are not the skill sets. Instead, it's how the top players think. It's how they go about winning. It's their method. It's how they work the point. It's their vision and plan, their long view, often thinking several shots ahead versus just reacting. I think this is the case in pickleball—that what separates the very good from the best is the difference between how they think.

Beginners don't play with a plan. Instead, they react. They try to win the rally with every shot they take. So they go for a fast serve, a fast return of serve…a fast every shot. In contrast, in advanced play, almost every shot following the return of serve will be a soft shot designed to land in the kitchen. An analogous beginner player in volleyball would seek to hit a winner from deep in the court rather than working to set up a spike.

The intermediate player may recognize the importance of getting fully forward quickly, but he or she will still try to do too much too quickly. When an intermediate player gets up to the line, he or she quickly goes for a risky shot.

The 5.0-rated player realizes that it's usually unwise to try to win the rally before getting fully forward. Once at the nonvolley zone (NVZ) line, the 5.0-rated player knows it's best to bide your time in a dinking exchange and wait patiently for a good opportunity before making an aggressive move.

Rally length and hit count data bear this out. In beginner play, most rallies end with five or fewer shots. Of course some of these rallies end quickly due to flubs and mis-hits. However, poor strategy is another contributor. Rallies involving the 3.5–4.0 skill level last a bit longer and have a few more hits, on average, than the beginner rallies do. Many of these rallies end due to poor shot choices and strategy. However, at the 5.0 skill level, not only do you see the skill and athleticism, but you also observe the patience, smart play, and withhold of attack until the right opportunity presents. Dinking exchanges can often go on for ten or more shots.

Recall the old saying, "Never interfere with an opponent while he's in the process of destroying himself." There's application for this rule in pickleball. Rather than taking risks with aggression, very often the best strategy is to simply continue to return the ball to your opponent. Under such a strategy, an impatient or less-skilled opponent will usually be the first to fault. Of course this doesn't mean that you give your opponent shots that provide advantage.

I know that some opponents have used such a strategy against me. I find that when I lose games to 5.0-level players, I usually feel like I've lost through my own errors. Indeed, the great players win most of their points against me not by making better shots but by simply waiting for me to make errors. Many of these errors are from trying to do too much too quickly.

Trying for Too Much Too Quickly and with Too Poor of a Setup

Most 4.0 level and below players try for too much too quickly and with too poor of a setup. They try to do too much with their serve and the return of serve. They try to go too close to the sideline. They try for too much angle, for example, a sharp crosscourt or a crosscourt to a sideline. They go for more power than is necessary. On keep-them-back shots, they go too deep. On smash shots, they go out of bounds from trying too much angle or too much depth. They start a fastball fight with a ball that is too low. They dink too deep, thereby giving their opponents a ball in the air. Rather than sticking with dinking, they attempt to lob. When they lob, they go for too much depth. The end result is that they lose too many rallies from the resulting trying-to-do-too-much errors. It's frustrating to play with a partner who repeatedly makes errors from trying to do too much as just described.

As a starting point, I encourage you to follow the formula described in this book, which is summarized below:

1. When serving, focus first on not faulting. If you are having trouble, hit slow and aim for the center of the box.

2. When returning the serve, hit to the opponent who has the poorest capability with the critical third shot. Return the serve with a semilob if necessary so you are fully in place at the NVZ line on time before the third shot comes across the net.

3. For a third shot, use the drop shot into the kitchen so long as your opponents are fully forward as they should be. If they are not at the line as they should be, hit toward the left-heel target of the deeper player. If your third shot is a little high, you may have to make a second or third drop shot attempt to enable getting fully forward. Be patient and avoid the temptation to blast the defensive wall. Remember, if you have to hit up on the ball, hit softly.

4. When fielding the third shot, stay fully forward, reach in, and volley the shot back, playing the keep-them-back shot, being careful not to give the opponent a volley shot.

5. If the third shot drops into the kitchen and if your opponents are still not up to the NVZ line, continue to play keep-them-back shots going low to the deeper player's backhand.

6. Once all players are fully forward, resolve that you'll be patient with the dinking process. Stay compressed, remain pinned to the NVZ line, and avoid backing up or making unnecessary foot movements. Volley dink shots back instead of backing up to let them bounce. Try to keep the dink shots

directed to player backhands. Stress your opponents, but remember that staying in the point is more important than going for a risky winner. Avoid issuing a fastball unless the ball is above the height of the net. If you choose to go fast, go to a good target, such as a point that forces a reach-out or a paddle flip.

As you can probably see right now, the basic strategy of pickleball can be summed up in just a few sentences: get your team fully forward as quickly as possible, and keep the other team back as long as possible. If you have to hit up on the ball, which is almost always, hit soft shots designed to bounce before being returned. If all players get fully forward, keep the ball low and soft (dink it) until a put-away opportunity arises.

Chapter 16 Quiz

Q1: You say that a person will likely never develop the at-the-line style of play to a high level unless he or she plays against opponents who are good at-the-line players. The problem is that I feel snubbed when I try to play with the good at-the-line players. How can I get accepted into this circle?

A1: This is a great question. I've been through this myself. For many months before being accepted, I was an "in-betweener" seeking to move from social play to at-the-line play. Here's my advice. First, make sure you belong in this group. Make sure you are a top player in your current group before attempting to move up. You should not be flubbing rather easy shots. You should be able to make a hundred or more consecutive alternating fore-hand and backhand volley shots against a practice wall without faulting. However, the most important thing is playing smart. If you are not going to play the at-the-line style of play, then do not attempt to join the at-the-line players. For example, after returning a serve, you must get fully to the NVZ line on time, every time. If you are on the serving team, you must attempt third shot drop shots instead of routinely giving the net players a shot that can be volleyed back. Whenever you are facing a team at the net and you must hit up on the ball, which is almost always, you should be trying to hit your shots into the kitchen. You must delay aggression until you have a high ball that allows a put away shot. So, you need to have a good drop shot and

solid dinking capability. You can develop both either with a practice partner or with wall practice. If you continue to get clobbered when playing with
this group, perform drills and wall practice until you can become competitive. I do not attempt to intrude on top level play. If I'm a 4.0-rated player, I
will seek to play with 4.0- or 4.5-rated players, but I will not intrude on the
5.0-rated players.

CHAPTER 17—ADVANCED STRATEGY: STACKING

The stacking player arrangement strategy is generally used only in tournament play. Rarely is it utilized in social play, except when players are practicing for tournament play. The stacking player arrangement strategy keeps the same player (player A) in the ad court for all rallies and keeps the same player (player B) in the deuce court for all rallies.

I'm not going to go over the mechanics and procedure for the full-stacking (stacking when serving and receiving) and half-stacking (stacking for only one of the two: serving or receiving) methodologies. You can find the procedure with diagrams and videos at many places on the web.

Instead, I'll talk about when and how to use the stacking strategy.

When you have a left-handed player playing with a right-handed player, it's usually desirable to have both forehands in the middle all the time, both when serving and receiving. So the left-handed player will be assigned to the deuce (even) court, and the right-handed player will be assigned to the ad (odd) court in the stacking arrangement. Many rallies end when the ball gets a little too high. This arrangement ensures any time a ball in the center region of the court gets too high, a forehand will smash it.

When you have a player with poor mobility playing with a partner with great mobility, assign the player with the poor mobility to the deuce court, and assign the player with the good mobility to the ad court. This assumes the player with the good mobility is right-handed. Why? It's much easier for a right-handed player with good mobility to move and field a shot going diagonally right than it is for a right-handed player with good mobility to move and field a shot going diagonally left.

These and other strategies are shown in this figure.

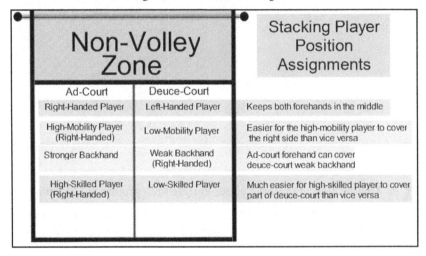

Non-Volley Zone		Stacking Player Position Assignments
Ad-Court	Deuce-Court	
Right-Handed Player	Left-Handed Player	Keeps both forehands in the middle
High-Mobility Player (Right-Handed)	Low-Mobility Player	Easier for the high-mobility player to cover the right side than vice versa
Stronger Backhand	Weak Backhand (Right-Handed)	Ad-court forehand can cover deuce-court weak backhand
High-Skilled Player (Right-Handed)	Low-Skilled Player	Much easier for high-skilled player to cover part of deuce-court than vice versa

Figure 17-1. Player position assignments when stacking

CHAPTER 18–MOVING FROM GOOD TO GREAT

Whether you are talking about golf, tennis, professional football, or any other sport, achieving greatness usually requires good coaching and instruction. You also need focused and goal-oriented practice and drills to perfect skills and shots. A helpful tool for this is a ball machine. You also need measurement and assessment of gaps and progress. Tools include video analysis and statistics. Finally, you need adjustments by the coach based on the outcomes and remaining gaps. Usually, the development process is a continuous cycle of (1) instruction on what to do, (2) practice, (3) evaluation/gap assessment, (4) adjustments, and (5) repeat the cycle. As common sense as all of this is, most players do not do any of it. As a consequence, they make only incremental improvements, if any.

Instruction/Get Expert Help

Almost all great players in every sport have coaches. Certainly, this applies to tennis and golf. A good coach can likely spot and address your worst faults in just a couple of hours. In other activities I've been involved in, the money I spent on private lessons was money well spent. A coach can help you bypass the trial-and-error process and get around beginner mistakes so you can quickly get to doing things right. I realize that coaches can be expensive and are not always available. In the absence of a coach, you may have to read books, watch videos, and seek the advice of the best players in your area.

Practice/Drills

Once your coach shows you what to do, you need to practice it. In chapter 5, I said that players at all levels will benefit much more from practice time than playing time. This rule applies to almost all sports. Especially in tennis and golf, the pros use their precious time not to play a game, but rather to practice shots and perform drills. Whether in tennis, golf, or pickleball, to improve shot-making skills, you must perform the same shot repeatedly. I'm not going to go over all the procedures for the various drills. Instead, I'm just going to list some of the drills I think are the most important. Most can be performed with just one partner.

The third shot (drop shot) drill. I gave the procedure for this drill earlier. This is about the most important and most difficult skill to learn in pickleball.

Dinking practice. You must reduce flubs and learn to steer the ball and keep it low.

Dink of an incoming fastball. You could use a partner or ball machine. Learn to dink or make an angled dink of an incoming fastball.

Overhead fake smash/dink. You could use a partner or ball machine. Learn to fake a smash, doing an overhead dink instead.

Offensive surprise lobs. You need to practice the disguise and touch required to get a trajectory that is high enough without being too short or too long.

Judging out-balls. You could use a partner or ball machine. You need to develop the calibration that keeps you from hitting out-balls.

Fast-game practice. This works best for four players. However, if you have just one partner, start by dinking back and forth with your partner using just one side of the court. You get a point for each time you start a fastball fight and win it. You lose a point for each time you start a fastball fight and lose it. Soon you will learn when to start a fight and when not to.

Single-side singles. Split the court in half along the court center line so you have a rectangle that is ten feet wide by forty-four feet long. Play singles on this half of the court only. This encourages use of the third shot (drop shot) and the at-the-line style of play. I prefer to play this against the best players I can find. Often, I play it as a warm-up or while I'm waiting for a regular doubles game.

Assessment/Measurement

A coach and a video camera can help here. It's tough to try to collect data while you are playing. A partner could help with this. As a starting point, here's key data you need:

- Service fault rate (percentage). Even for low–intermediate players, this should be under 5 percent.
- Return-of-serve fault rate (percentage). Even for low–intermediate players, this should be under 7 percent.
- Starting with the third shot, the number of shots you hit that allowed your opponent to volley back. Recall that you should avoid giving your opponent a ball in the air (a ball he or she can volley back) unless it's a shot designed to defeat reaction time.
- When on the serving team, percentage of the rallies where you are able to get fully to the nonvolley zone (NVZ) line. Work toward getting this above 75 percent.
- When on the serving team, percentage of your third shot attempts that lead directly to a loss of the rally (too high or into the net). Initially, this number will be high: maybe near 50 percent.
- When returning the serve, percentage of the time that you allow a third shot or any shot afterward to bounce outside your kitchen area before you hit it. There is no reason this number should not be below 5 percent.
- Number of your shots going out of bounds.
- Number of your shots going into the net (especially from using too much power).
- Number of dink flubs into the net.
- Number of untouched down-the-middle shots that your team allowed.

I personally do not like the very broad unforced error statistic, since it does not provide specific, actionable information. Instead, you need to collect data that includes shots and their specific outcomes.

Compete

One of the best ways to move from being good to being great is to compete in tournaments or league play. I realize that most players will dismiss this advice immediately, with their reaction being, "No way! I'm not good enough." However, I can assure you that playing against and competing against great players is a valuable and necessary path to achieving greatness. Likely, nothing will improve your game more than the decision to begin competing. Competing is a good way to measure where you stand and how much you are improving.

For most folks, their attitude toward competing is, "I'll get clobbered. So why do it?" Most tournaments have beginner, intermediate, and advanced brackets. For me, the most important goal of competing is not to win a prize but to get better. You become a better player by playing better players. You learn from them—both what to do and not do. Only when you play against great players will you learn to execute the strategy described in this book. Only when I left the social pickleball arena to crack into the advanced arena did my game make a big step change improvement. I'm convinced that the best way to further improve my game is to continue to play against the best players I can find.

I can't travel to tournaments as much as I'd like to. However, I participate in league play just about every week. The league play is essentially a tournament, and almost all the best players in the area participate.

NOTES

I've used many statistics throughout the book. Statistics are based on samples. Even large and representative samples can only approximate the whole population. This is called sampling error. So all my statistics have some level of error. Unless otherwise noted, most of the data comes from tournaments involving top 5.0-rated players. I've personally recorded many hours of social and tournament play at many different player-rating levels. This has allowed me to compare statistics between, say, 4.0- and 5.0-rated players. A few other folks have collected and published pickleball statistical data. I've used some of this data in this book as well. Hopefully other pickleball-data collectors will contribute to the data pile and help better nail down the exact percentages.

AUTHOR BIOGRAPHY

Joe Baker is an enthusiastic pickleball player and teacher. His YouTube videos on pickleball strategy have received more than 300,000 views to date. His video fans have been calling for a book to bring all this information together in one place. This book is the result.

Baker received his bachelor's degree in mechanical engineering from North Carolina State University and worked thirty-five years for the DuPont Corporation. He is semiretired and now lives in Richmond, Virginia. Learn more at www.pickleballhelp.blogspot.com.

Made in United States
North Haven, CT
23 December 2023

46535285R00089